GOD
THE ENOUGH

Every Day Light for
Your Journey

© 2001
Text copyright by Selwyn Hughes
All rights reserved
Printed in Belgium

0–8054–2372–9

Published by Broadman & Holman Publishers, Nashville, Tennessee
Cover & Interior Design: Identity Design Inc., Dallas, Texas

Dewey Decimal Classification: 242.2
Subject Heading: DEVOTIONAL EXERCISES

Every Day Light™
CWR, Waverley Abbey House, Waverley Lane, Farnham, Surrey GU9 8EP

Material taken from *Every Day with Jesus*, God—The Enough 1996

SELWYN HUGHES

is the founder of CWR (Crusade for
World Revival) and the author of *Every Day
with Jesus*, a best-selling daily devotional
resource read by more than 500,000
around the world each day. He is the author
of the best-selling books *Every Day Light*,
Water for the Soul, and *Light for the Path*.
An internationally known British theologian
and commentator, Hughes lives in Farnham,
Surrey near London, England.

The Selwyn Hughes Signature Series is a collection
of elegant books each featuring daily devotionals with
Bible passages, Selwyn Hughes' own notes and
commentary, a prayer for daily meditation,
plus room for journal entries.

Signature Series

SELWYN HUGHES

GOD

THE ENOUGH

Every Day Light for
Your Journey

BROADMAN
& HOLMAN
PUBLISHERS

NASHVILLE, TENNESSEE

THE ALL-SUFFICIENT ONE

On one occasion the good Lord said,
"Everything is going to be all right."
On another, "You will see for yourself
that every sort of thing will be
all right." In these two sayings the
soul discerns various meanings.
One is that he wants us to know
that not only does he care for great
and noble things, but equally for
little and small, lowly and simple
things as well. This is his meaning:
"*Every*-thing will be all right."
We are to know that the least thing
will not be forgotten.

— Julian of Norwich

A New Name

"When Abram was ninety-nine years old, *the Lord appeared to him and said, 'I am God Almighty*; walk before me and be blameless. I will confirm my covenant between me and you and will greatly increase your numbers.' Abram fell facedown, and God said to him, 'As for me, this is my covenant with you: You will be the father of many nations. No longer will you be called Abram; your name will be Abraham, for I have made you a father of many nations. I will make you very fruitful; I will make nations of you, and kings will come from you. I will establish my covenant as an everlasting covenant between me and you and your descendants after you for the generations to come, to be your God and the God of your descendants after you.'"

Genesis 17:1–7

The term *God—the Enough* is a working equivalent of the Hebrew name for God—*El-Shaddai*—which appears in our text for today as "God Almighty." When God introduced Himself by a different name in the Old Testament, it was always to reveal a new and exciting aspect of Himself. The revelation recorded in the passage we have read today came after Abram and Sarai had attempted to obtain the promised offspring by using a surrogate mother. The name is sometimes translated as "the All-Sufficient One" or "the Nourisher of His People." But the term I like best is "God—the Enough." Abram and Sarai were to discover that when it comes to bringing His purposes to pass, the Almighty needs no help from His creatures. He is *enough*.

A Question to Ponder

The question I would like to pose and then answer in the weeks that lie ahead is simply this: Is God enough? If you were stripped of friends, possessions, and health, would God be enough for you to carry on? That question is one with which all of us must come to grips. Is God relevant—or are we just kidding ourselves? It's one thing to read the words in Scripture, but are they a reality in our daily lives? Is God all we need? I believe He is. How about you? I hope through these meditations you will come to agree with me that the eternal God *is* sufficient for us—no matter what situation we find ourselves in.

O God my Father, may I be encouraged by
the reassuring revelation that whatever situation
I find myself in, You are enough. May I know
this not only in theory but in practice also.
In Jesus' Name I pray. Amen.

IS GOD ENOUGH?

At Least Enough

"Then the LORD answered Job out of the storm. He said: 'Who is this that darkens my counsel with words without knowledge? Brace yourself like a man; I will question you, and you shall answer me. *Where were you when I laid the earth's foundation? Tell me, if you understand.* Who marked off its dimensions? Surely you know! Who stretched a measuring line across it? On what were its footings set, or who laid its cornerstone—while the morning stars sang together and all the angels shouted for joy? Who shut up the sea behind doors when it burst forth from the womb, when I made the clouds its garment and wrapped it in thick darkness, when I fixed limits for it and set its doors and bars in place, when I said, "This far you may come and no farther; here is where your proud waves halt"?'"

Job 38:1–11

We said yesterday that a good working equivalent of the name *El-Shaddai* is God—the Enough. But one Hebrew professor I heard lecturing on this subject took exception to this translation, arguing that it does not truly reflect the meaning of the original language. He maintained the thought underlying the term *El-Shaddai* is that of superabundance. God is not just enough, he claimed, but always *more* than enough. Take the vastness of the universe, he said. It is conceivable that the world could have been constructed on a lesser scale. Was there a need to make it so big? Why then is it so large? God's purpose (so he believed) was to impress upon us that He is gloriously sufficient, extravagantly plentiful—*more* than enough.

Confidence in the Creator

In my view, the point he made was a good one. Certainly this was the message being given by the Almighty to Job in our passage today. God was saying in effect: "Take a look at the vastness of the universe. Doesn't it strike you that if I can put all this together and sustain it then I am able to hold you in the midst of all your troubles?" He was trying to convey to Job that the greater his wonder at the creative might of his Maker and the larger his vision of the vastness of the universe, the more confident he should be not only of the power that brought it into being but of the Creator's ability to uphold him in his difficulties.

Though I take the Hebrew scholar's point that God—the Enough is not the most precise translation of the term *El-Shaddai*, isn't it comforting to know that however much more than enough God is to meet and match our human need, He is always *at least* enough. He is nothing less than that.

My Father and my God, give me, I pray, a new comprehension of the fact that You are unchangingly adequate, eternally sufficient, abidingly plentiful. You are "the Enough" in creation and enough for me also. I am deeply thankful. Amen.

GOD IS GLORIOUSLY SUFFICIENT, EXTRAVAGANTLY PLENTIFUL.

"PENSIONERS OF PROVIDENCE"

"The LORD is faithful to all his promises and loving toward all he has made. The LORD upholds all those who fall and lifts up all who are bowed down. The eyes of all look to you, and you give them their food at the proper time. *You open your hand and satisfy the desires of every living thing.* The LORD is righteous in all his ways and loving toward all he has made. The LORD is near to all who call on him, to all who call on him in truth. He fulfills the desires of those who fear him; he hears their cry and saves them. The LORD watches over all who love him, but all the wicked he will destroy."

Psalm 145:13b–20

Clearly, as we have seen, God is "the Enough" in the realm of creation. Take a walk in the woods ere winter sets in, and what do you see? The ground is strewn with thousands of seeds and nuts, each capable of reproducing the plant or tree from which it fell. Why such extravagance? Is it not to impress upon our minds the lavishness of a God who is more than enough? There is in nature a wondrous prodigality, a superabundance of created things. Yes, God is "the Enough" in creation.

Debtors to God

The text before us today draws our attention to the fact that God is "the Enough" in the realm of providence also.

Each one of us is in debt to God for the air we breathe and the food we eat. And, as we discover from the well-known verse in Romans chapter 8—"in all things God works for the good of those who love him" (v. 28)—a special providence governs the lives of those who are His redeemed children. Isaac Watts conveys this thought most beautifully in his famous hymn:

Thy providence is kind and large,
Both man and beast Thy bounty share;
The whole creation is Thy charge,
But saints are Thy peculiar care.

Though we may not often reflect on this fact (more's the pity), every one of us, every moment of the day, is utterly dependent on the benevolence of God. For all our material needs God has furnished an abundant supply. Let this thought engage your attention this day: quite literally, as someone has described it, "We are the pensioners of Providence."

O Father, forgive me that so often I forget the fact that I am a "pensioner of Providence." I am not so much the owner of things as the recipient. Impress upon me the truth that every moment of my existence on this earth I am a dependent being. Were You not there, I would not be here. Amen.

GOD IS "THE ENOUGH" IN CREATION.

GIVING GRACE THE CREDIT

"... last of all he appeared to me also, as to one abnormally born. For I am the least of the apostles and do not even deserve to be called an apostle, because I persecuted the church of God. But by the grace of God I am what I am, and his grace to me was not without effect. No, *I worked harder than all of them—yet not I, but the grace of God that was with me.* Whether, then, it was I or they, this is what we preach, and this is what you believed."

1 Corinthians 15:8–11

Wonderful though it may be to reflect on how God is the Enough in the realms of creation and providence, what is even more wonderful is this: God is "the Enough" in the realm of grace. This, to my way of thinking, is the most wonderful thing of all.

Definitions of Grace

What is grace? To many people "grace" is simply something you say before a meal, but in its biblical usage it has a far greater and wider meaning than that. W. E. Vine, the famous Greek scholar, defined it like this: "Grace, the divine quality of grace, is goodwill, friendliness, favorable regard, extravagant loving-kindness." One of the best definitions of *grace* I have heard is this: "Grace is the strength God gives us to live as His

Son lived when He was here upon the earth." God's grace was enough for Jesus; it is enough also for us.

Paul testified in our passage today of how he surpassed the other apostles, when he said: "I worked harder than all of them." It sounds as if Paul was boasting here, but he immediately qualified the statement by adding: "yet not I, but the grace of God that was with me." In this age, when there is so much emphasis on self-achievement, you don't hear many Christians saying something similar. When did you last hear a believer who had reached the pinnacle of his or her career declare: "Don't be impressed with what I have achieved. It has all come about through the grace of God that has been at work in me"? This idea of giving God's grace the credit is one that needs to be stressed in today's ego-centered climate. Where would you and I be today were it not for the grace of God? I shudder to think.

O God, help me give grace the credit for all the achievements of my life. Far too often I have attributed my success to the talents I possess instead of giving the credit to the One who, through grace, gave me those talents. Forgive me and help me. In Jesus' Name I pray. Amen.

"GRACE IS THE STRENGTH GOD GIVES US TO LIVE AS HIS SON LIVED WHEN HE WAS HERE UPON THE EARTH."

WHEN BEREFT OF HUMAN LOVE

"Yet I am always with you; you hold me by my right hand. You guide me with your counsel, and afterward you will take me into glory. Whom have I in heaven but you? And earth has nothing I desire besides you. *My flesh and my heart may fail, but God is the strength of my heart and my portion forever.* Those who are far from you will perish; you destroy all who are unfaithful to you. But as for me, it is good to be near God. I have made the Sovereign LORD my refuge; I will tell of all your deeds."

Psalm 73:23–28

None, I am sure, will doubt that God is enough in the realm of creation and in the realm of providence. But is He enough in the realm of grace? Can His grace be so active in our lives that it enables us to come through *every* problem we face? And not only come through, but come through victoriously? I believe it can.

Consider a problem facing many in today's world, the problem of being bereft of the love that comes from an intimate human relationship. Those who are divorced, separated, or who have lost a spouse through death, will know instantly what I mean. And those who are single for whatever reason and have no close relationship with another will know what I mean also. A divorced woman tearfully expressed it like this: "I have a good relationship with the Lord, but He cannot literally put His arms around me, buy me flowers, plant a kiss on my lips, or snuggle up to me in bed on a cold night." Over and over again and in various forms I have had this question put to me by those who lack a close loving human relationship: Can God draw so close to me that His presence becomes a substitute for the love derived from an intimate relationship?

Compensation from God

This might surprise you, but my answer has always been "No." God is not a physical being and therefore cannot, in that sense, be a substitute for a wife, husband, boyfriend, or girlfriend. He does not pretend that will be the case. But He can *compensate* to such a degree that although a close human relationship may be missing and keenly mourned, nevertheless one can still function effectively in life and feel fulfilled in the deepest parts of one's being.

O God, help me understand that while You do not pretend to be a substitute for a person with whom one can have a close, loving relationship, You more than compensate for the lack of human love. I may feel the loss of human affection, but because of Your presence in my soul, I am not devastated by it. Thank You, my Father. Amen.

GOD IS NOT A PHYSICAL BEING.

THE FOUR LOVES

"For this reason I kneel before the Father, from whom his whole family in heaven and on earth derives its name. I pray that out of his glorious riches he may strengthen you with power through his Spirit in your inner being, so that Christ may dwell in your hearts through faith. *And I pray that you, being rooted and established in love, may* have power, together with all the saints, to grasp how wide and long and high and deep is the love of Christ, and to *know this love that surpasses knowledge*—that you may be filled to the measure of all the fullness of God."

Ephesians 3:14–19

Part of what one feels deep in the soul when one is bereft of human love is a sense of loneliness. There are, of course, degrees of loneliness. A man may be temporarily separated from his wife, or a wife from her husband, by reason of circumstances, and feelings of loneliness set in. But these feelings are tempered by the knowledge that a reunion will soon take place. Others have to face the fact that their separation from a spouse is permanent, as in the case of death or divorce. For these, the feelings of loneliness run much deeper. Concerning the divorced, the separated, the bereaved, and those for whom there might be little hope of another legitimate intimate human relationship, one must again ask: Is the great *El-Shaddai* able to succour them in their loneliness?

The Resources of God's Love

C. S. Lewis, in his book *The Four Loves*, takes the four Greek words for love—*agape, philia, storge,* and *eros*—and explains how each differs from the other. *Agape* describes the kind of love found in the heart of the Deity—unconditional love, the love that does not depend on any answering love in the heart of the one it loves. *Philia* is the love expressed between friends. *Storge* is the love seen in a family. And *eros* is intense physical love, the kind of love shared between a man and a woman in marriage. Some reading these words will know nothing of erotic love, or family love, and perhaps little even of the love found in friendship. This then raises the question again: Can those who find themselves bereft of intimate human relationships live a fulfilled and satisfying life? Providing they make use of the resources found in God, they can.

O Father, Bearer of every pain that plagues
Your children, draw close to me in moments
of loneliness so that, notwithstanding the pain,
I can still function and move through life,
sharing Your love with everyone I meet.
In Christ's Name I ask it. Amen.

THE KIND OF LOVE FOUND IN THE HEART OF THE
DEITY IS UNCONDITIONAL.

"JESUS WILL COME...."

"Submit yourselves, then, to God. Resist the devil, and he will flee from you. *Come near to God and he will come near to you.* Wash your hands, you sinners, and purify your hearts, you double-minded. Grieve, mourn and wail. Change your laughter to mourning and your joy to gloom. Humble yourselves before the Lord, and he will lift you up. Brothers, do not slander one another. Anyone who speaks against his brother or judges him speaks against the law and judges it. When you judge the law, you are not keeping it, but sitting in judgment on it. There is only one Lawgiver and Judge, the one who is able to save and destroy. But you—who are you to judge your neighbor?"

James 4:7–12

Today we ask ourselves: How does the great *El-Shaddai* go about the task of sustaining those who need His grace and strength when bereft of an intimate human relationship? There are two ways: He makes them deeply aware of His presence and then helps them to minister to others.

Take the first: *He makes them deeply aware of His presence.* Our Lord, to some degree, must have felt lonely all His days, but the loneliness He felt was caused by those around Him, not His heavenly Father. Sometimes He would slip away from the disciples in order to be alone with God. These were His feast times, when He enjoyed most fully the companionship of His Father. To delight in the presence of God, to live in conscious nearness to the Almighty, to spend one's days in reverent intimacy with Him is to live indeed. Thomas à Kempis expressed it like this: "Jesus will come unto thee and show thee His consolation, if thou prepare for Him a worthy abode within thee. When Jesus is present all is good and nothing seems difficult. To know how to keep Jesus is great wisdom. Be thou humble and peaceable, devout and quiet, and Jesus will stay with thee."

Receiving Grace

Note the words: *"if thou prepare for Him a worthy abode within thee."* The great *El-Shaddai* will supply the grace needed and will fill the soul with His presence, but it must be received. Always remember, if one lacks a thrilling sense of God's presence, it is not God's fault. The problem is not one of giving but of receiving. Know this: when one is bereft of human love, He will come close.

O Father, how thankful I am that there is no situation—loneliness included—in which You are unable to help. I draw near to You, and You draw near to me. How simple, yet how sublime. Thank You, my Father. Amen.

"WHEN JESUS IS PRESENT ALL IS GOOD AND NOTHING SEEMS DIFFICULT."

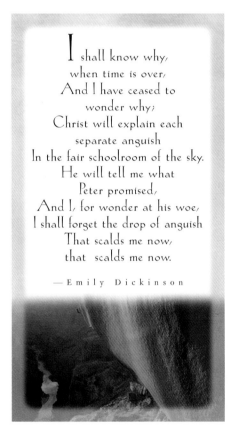

I shall know why,
when time is over,
And I have ceased to
wonder why;
Christ will explain each
separate anguish
In the fair schoolroom of the sky.
He will tell me what
Peter promised,
And I, for wonder at his woe,
I shall forget the drop of anguish
That scalds me now,
that scalds me now.

— Emily Dickinson

_____

_____

_____

_____

_____

_____

_____

_____

_____

_____

_____

_____

_____

_____

_____

_____

_____

_____

GRACE IS FLOWING LIKE A RIVER

Sin and grace are bound to each other. We do not even have a knowledge of sin unless we have already experienced the unity of life, which is grace. And conversely, we could not grasp the meaning of grace without having experienced the separation of life, which is sin.

— Paul Tillich

NOT WORTH

MENTIONING

"Love must be sincere. Hate what is evil; cling to what is good. Be devoted to one another in brotherly love. Honor one another above yourselves. *Never be lacking in zeal, but keep your spiritual fervor, serving the Lord.* Be joyful in hope, patient in affliction, faithful in prayer. Share with God's people who are in need. Practice hospitality."

Romans 12:9–13

We said yesterday that God sustains those who find themselves bereft of human love in two ways: by making them aware of His presence and by helping them minister to others. He cannot provide what we lack in human contact, but He can impart such a sense of His presence that though it does not remove the ache for human love, it enables us to function effectively and contribute to the interests of His kingdom.

The Presence of Grace

Look with me now at the second of His ways: *He helps us minister to others.* Lonely people can very quickly shrink into their shell, become critical, self-pitying, and unconsciously drive people away. I know many lacking human affection who have nevertheless so cultivated their relationship with the Lord that His grace and love spill over into the lives of everyone they meet.

The Greek word *charis*, which is translated in the New Testament as "grace," also means "charm." The grace of our Lord Jesus Christ adds charm to our hearts. Or so it should. Who hasn't noticed a couple fall in love and observed how radiant they become? It is the same with those who are deeply in love with Jesus. His love irradiates human nature and heightens its attractiveness. Love begets love. One person put it like this: "A sublime feeling of God's presence comes about me at times which makes inward solitariness a trifle not worth talking about." What a glorious testimony.

If you lack a close human relationship then do not, I beg you, lapse into self-pity and say: "Poor me." You have the friendship of God. Rejoice in it and share it with others.

Father, I see that those who live close to You
are infected with Your desire for fellowship.
Help me live in close communion with You and
make me an expert in ministering to others.
In Christ's Name I pray. Amen.

LOVE BEGETS LOVE.

THE CHANGELESS CENTER

"'*I the LORD do not change.* So you, O descendants of Jacob, are not destroyed. Ever since the time of your forefathers you have turned away from my decrees and have not kept them. Return to me, and I will return to you,' says the LORD Almighty. 'But you ask, "How are we to return?" Will a man rob God? Yet you rob me. But you ask, "How do we rob you?" In tithes and offerings. You are under a curse—the whole nation of you— because you are robbing me. Bring the whole tithe into the storehouse, that there may be food in my house. Test me in this,' says the LORD Almighty, 'and see if I will not throw open the floodgates of heaven and pour out so much blessing that you will not have room enough for it.'"

Malachi 3:6–10

We turn now to think about another question that relates to our theme: Is God enough when we face the changes that life inevitably brings us? Many of us find it difficult to cope with change and strenuously resist it. We do the same things over and over again, and it all becomes a habit. Some find change not only difficult but deeply disturbing. And yet life *is* change. There is nothing changeless about life except change. One observer of human nature put it like this: "The familiar is like a pair of shoes that have been well worn and are extremely comfortable; the unfamiliar is like a pebble in the same shoe making it difficult to walk along life's way."

Resistance to Change

The British have a reputation for not liking change. This is why they cling to their old traditions. It is not so much that they value tradition but they abhor change. A visitor to Britain tells how he was invited to have a meal with a friend, a member of Parliament, in a private dining room in the House of Commons. During the meal someone put his head around the door and asked: "Anybody going home?" The friend explained to him that this rather strange question dated back to the days when members of Parliament risked being beaten up by thugs, so they were escorted home. It was language left over from the past.

Is God enough when we are called upon to face major changes in our lives? Perhaps you are facing a significant change at this moment. If so, then listen: the great *El-Shaddai* enables us to cope with change by providing Himself as the changeless center of our lives. We can cope more easily with outward change when we have the changeless One within.

My Father and my God, how reassuring
it is to know that whatever changes take place
around me, I am linked to the One who is
changeless. Help me live in the light of this fact.
In Christ's Name I pray. Amen.

THERE IS NOTHING CHANGELESS ABOUT LIFE EXCEPT CHANGE.

GRACE ABOUNDING

"Just as the result of one trespass was condemnation for all men, so also the result of one act of righteousness was justification that brings life for all men. For just as through the disobedience of the one man the many were made sinners, so also through the obedience of the one man the many will be made righteous. The law was added so that the trespass might increase. *But where sin increased, grace increased all the more,* so that, just as sin reigned in death, so also grace might reign through righteousness to bring eternal life through Jesus Christ our Lord."

Romans 5:18–21

We turn now to what is probably the most important question in connection with the theme we are pursuing: Is God enough to deal with the issues that arise from the fact of human sin? Or to put it another way: Is there enough grace in the heart of God to meet and overcome the difficulties created by evil? Again I say, there is!

The Sin Problem

Sin is without doubt the biggest problem God has ever had to deal with. When we read the four Gospels we see something of the pain God has gone through in order to defeat sin and its consequences. They spell out in terms that are crystal clear how much anguish sin brought about in the heart of the Deity. The theologian Martin Kähler worded it like this: "The four Gospels are shaped as passion narratives with long introductions. At the heart of each Gospel is a pool of pain." Throughout the centuries, Christians have always evaluated the horror of sin by the suffering needed to atone for it. Cornelius Plantinga, in his book *Not the Way It's Supposed to Be*, spells out the issue in these poignant words: "The ripping and writhing of a body on a cross, the bizarre metaphysical maneuver of using death to defeat death, the urgency of the summons to human beings to ally themselves with the events of Christ and with the Person of those events, and then to make that Person and those events the center of their lives—these tell us the main human trouble is desperately difficult to fix, even for God, and that sin is the longest running of all human emergencies."

What is God's answer to sin? "The suffering of Christ," you say. Yes, that was how sin was overcome. But what prompted that suffering? What motivated it? It was grace. Grace increasing, abounding, and sufficient. Hallelujah!

Father, I bow in wonder before the fact of Your amazing grace. Nothing can distance it or outshine it. Thank You, dear Lord, that I am a recipient of that grace. Amen.

"AT THE HEART OF EACH GOSPEL IS A POOL OF PAIN."

DECISION DAY

"But now a righteousness from God, apart from law, has been made known, to which the Law and the Prophets testify. This righteousness from God comes through faith in Jesus Christ to all who believe. There is no difference, *for all have sinned* and fall short of the glory of God, *and are justified freely by his grace* through the redemption that came by Christ Jesus. God presented him as a sacrifice of atonement, through faith in his blood. He did this to demonstrate his justice, because in his forbearance he had left the sins committed beforehand unpunished—he did it to demonstrate his justice at the present time, so as to be just and the one who justifies those who have faith in Jesus."

Romans 3: 21–26

The point we are making as we come to grips with the tragic fact of sin is this: no matter how many problems sin has introduced into the universe, they are no match for the grace of God. I like what one theologian says about grace: "It is not the attribute of love alone that has matched itself against sin, but grace. For grace is love reaching down. *In fact, it could be said it is sin that transforms love into grace*" (emphasis mine). Can you see what he means? Had sin not entered the universe, then neither the angels nor humanity would ever have comprehended that part of God's nature that we describe as grace. We would have grasped it intellectually, of course, but not experientially. Our spiritual songs would have been of love, of power, of might and majesty—but not of grace.

Do You Know God's Grace?

D. L. Moody, the famous nineteenth-century American evangelist, told how one day he sat in his study meditating on the fact of God's grace. As he did so, he became so overwhelmed by the thought of sin giving rise to a new revelation of God that flinging aside his pen, he dashed into the street. Accosting the first man he met, he demanded, "Do you know 'grace'?" "Grace who?" was the surprised response. "*God's* grace, man," said the evangelist. "God's grace. Do you know *God's* grace?"

Permit me to ask you that same question: Do you know God's grace? Have you allowed it to reach into your soul and sweep away your sin? What a wonderful thought it is that no matter how deeply we may have fallen into sin, God's grace is able to get beneath it and lift us out of it, and it out of us. If you have not yet experienced God's grace in a saving way, then I urge you to pray this prayer:

O God my Father, I open my heart to
You right now and receive Jesus Christ as my
Lord and Savior. Forgive my sin, and by Your grace
change me through and through. You have done it
for multitudes of others—now do it for me.
In Jesus' Name I pray. Amen.

GRACE IS LOVE REACHING DOWN.

"LOVE...WITH A STAIN"

"Finally, brothers, good-by. Aim for perfection, listen to my appeal, be of one mind, live in peace. And the God of love and peace will be with you. Greet one another with a holy kiss. All the saints send their greetings. *May the grace of the Lord Jesus Christ, and the love of God,* and the fellowship of the Holy Spirit *be with you all.*"

2 Corinthians 13:11–14

When we speak of sin, we should always speak of it in the context of grace. To focus on sin without any reference to grace is to overlook the resolve and determination of God. God wants to return His creation to the state it was in before sin entered the world, and He will pay any price, within the bounds of His character, to achieve that. Human sin is stubborn, but not as stubborn as grace. And not half as persistent either, not half as ready to suffer. To speak of sin without referring to grace is to forget that the life, death, and resurrection of Jesus Christ is the only hope for victory over evil. Sin shouts to the universe: "Bad news." The Gospel shouts: "Good News."

The Gospel of Grace

However, we should not focus on grace without making mention of sin. And why? Because to talk about grace without focusing on why grace is needed is to trivialize the cross of our Lord Jesus Christ, to ignore the lives and endeavors of the saints throughout the ages, and to downplay the fact that God's grace always comes to us with the stain of blood upon it. Why do we think Christ was skewered to a Roman cross? Why the ripping and writhing on grim Golgotha? If we speak of grace without reference to these realities, without recognizing and acknowledging our own individual sin, we are doing something akin to taking a symphony and reducing it to a single note. When the Christian Church ignores sin, euphemizes it, or tones down its awful reality, then we are cutting the very nerve of the Gospel. Cornelius Platinga wrote: "Without the full disclosure of sin, the gospel of grace becomes impertinent, unnecessary and finally uninteresting." I agree.

Father, help me cherish the thought that grace is love with the stain of blood upon it. May I open the whole of my being to Your wondrous grace so that my life shows others what grace can do in a ransomed sinner. In Christ's Name I pray. Amen.

THE LIFE, DEATH, AND RESURRECTION OF JESUS CHRIST
IS THE ONLY HOPE FOR VICTORY OVER EVIL.

R U G G E D
L A N G U A G E

"As it is written: 'There is no one righteous, not even one; *there is no one who understands, no one who seeks God.* All have turned away, they have together become worthless; there is no one who does good, not even one.' 'Their throats are open graves; their tongues practice deceit.' 'The poison of vipers is on their lips.' 'Their mouths are full of cursing and bitterness.' 'Their feet are swift to shed blood; ruin and misery mark their ways, and the way of peace they do not know.' 'There is no fear of God before their eyes.'"

Romans 3:10–18

The matter of sin and grace does not seem to occupy the attention of modern-day Christians to anything like the same degree that it did our forefathers, generally speaking. One has only to read the literature of the past to see that the men and women of God in previous generations hated sin, feared it, grieved over it, and fled from it. As a child growing up in the forties, I heard as many sermons about sin as I did about grace. The impression I received was that I could not understand either without understanding both. Yet today, in some parts of the church, the subjects of sin and grace are not clearly expounded. If we fail to comprehend the full meaning of sin, then we will not understand the significance of grace.

The Issue of Sin

I am afraid that the new language of Zion fudges the issue of sin. One preacher, using what I consider to be legitimate hyperbole, says that it won't be too long before we hear confessionals taking this form: "Let us confess our problem with human relational dynamics, especially our feebleness in networking." Where sin is concerned, we don't speak out clearly, unlike our forefathers. We mumble. The word *sin* is used more frequently in secular society than it is in some church circles. An advertisement promoting a certain perfume calls it "My Sin." At my favorite restaurant the menu describes one dessert as "a sinful experience." The new measure for sin is calorific.

The words of another preacher sum up the situation: "If the church does not get back to focusing once again on the issues of sin and grace, then it won't be long before we hear the phrase not 'God be merciful to me a sinner,' but 'God be merciful to me a miscalculator.'"

O Father, awaken Your church to the realities of sin and grace. Forgive us that we make sin such a minor issue and see grace as something to be taken for granted. Save us from fudging these vital issues. In Christ's Name I pray. Amen.

TODAY, IN SOME PARTS OF THE CHURCH, THE SUBJECTS OF SIN AND GRACE ARE NOT CLEARLY EXPOUNDED.

CHEAP GRACE

"What shall we say, then? Shall we go on sinning so that grace may increase? By no means! We died to sin; how can we live in it any longer? Or don't you know that all of us who were baptized into Christ Jesus were baptized into his death? We were therefore buried with him through baptism into death in order that, just as Christ was raised from the dead through the glory of the Father, we too may live a new life. If we have been united with him like this in his death, we will certainly also be united with him in his resurrection. For we know that our old self was crucified with him so that the body of sin might be done away with, that we should no longer be slaves to sin — because anyone who has died has been freed from sin."

Romans 6:1–7

Today I would like to look with you at a question that is often posed when the subject of God's free and extravagant grace is discussed: Won't a strong emphasis on grace lead to an abuse of grace? Martyn Lloyd-Jones, in one of his books, made the point that the true preaching of the Gospel by grace alone always involves the possibility of this charge being raised. And this is the issue with which Paul deals in the passage we have read today.

Some argue that because our sin gives God the opportunity to show His grace, then the more we sin, the more God can demonstrate something that otherwise would remain hidden and untapped. Many preachers are aware that a sermon on the theme of grace is dangerous in the sense that it can easily be misunderstood. A number of people take advantage of the truth of grace to promote the erroneous idea that because God is a God of grace, then you can go on sinning as much as you like. Truth out of balance becomes error. Dietrich Bonhoeffer, the German theologian executed by the Nazis just before the end of World War II, was well-known for his criticism of those who emphasized grace to the exclusion of responsibility. When grace was preached without a corresponding emphasis on responsibility, he described it as "cheap grace."

Salvation by Grace

Salvation is by grace alone, but grace goes on to provide us with the power to live the way God requires. A true understanding of grace will not lead us to indulge in sin in order that grace may abound; instead, it will evoke in us this kind of thinking: *In the light of what God has done for me, what can I now do for Him?*

Dear Father, help me never to fall into the trap of thinking that because grace is so free and abundant, I need not take my sin seriously. Show me even more clearly that because I have died to sin I must no longer live therein. In Jesus' Name I pray. Amen.

I have nothing whereof
I may glory in my works:
I will therefore glory in
Christ. I will not glory
because I am righteous,
but because I am redeemed;
not because I am clear
of sin, but because my
sins are forgiven.

—Ambrose of Milan

_____

_____

_____

_____

_____

_____

_____

_____

_____

_____

_____

_____

_____

_____

_____

_____

_____

_____

_____

_____

_____

THE VALLEY
OF
THE SHADOW

For all that has been

—Thanks!

For all that shall be

—Yes!

— Dag Hammarskjöld

ABUNDANT GRACE

"Praise be to the God and Father of our Lord Jesus Christ, who has blessed us in the heavenly realms with every spiritual blessing in Christ. For he chose us in him before the creation of the world to be holy and blameless in his sight. In love he predestined us to be adopted as his sons through Jesus Christ in accordance with his pleasure and will—*to the praise of his glorious grace, which he has freely given us in the One he loves.* In him we have redemption through his blood, the forgiveness of sins, in accordance with the riches of God's grace that he lavished on us with all wisdom and understanding."

Ephesians 1:3–8

The point we have been making over the past few days is this: grace is more than a match for human sin. I wonder, am I talking to someone today who has committed some grievous sin and you question whether or not God can forgive you? The offence may be awful and very serious. You may be saying even now: Does God have enough grace to forgive this dreadful thing I have done? The answer is *yes.* Listen to the words of the great hymn writer Charles Wesley:

Plenteous grace with Thee is found,
Grace to cover all my sin.

Full Forgiveness

All my sin. There is nothing you have done that cannot be forgiven. Isn't that astonishing? Grace for the vilest, grace for the weakest, grace for the least, the last, and the lost.

Once, while in Nairobi, East Africa, a man grasped my hand and said: "I have committed all the sins in the book. I thought God would never forgive me. I have sinned against my wife, my daughter, my family, my employer, and God. You name it, I've done it. Tonight I heard you say that God could forgive *all* my sin. *All.* I have asked Him, and I know He has done so." Amazing. God is "the Enough" in creation, God is "the Enough" in providence, God is "the Enough" when we are bereft of human love, God is "the Enough" in the midst of life's great changes. But is He enough in grace? Millions of voices from all parts of the world today will echo the answer: Yes, He is enough. *More* than enough.

Father, I add my own testimony to that of the multitudes who pay tribute to Your grace. It's amazing. Help me show my gratitude not only in words but in deeds. May I display grace to others in my attitude, my disposition, my character. In Jesus' Name. Amen.

THERE IS NOTHING YOU HAVE DONE
THAT CANNOT BE FORGIVEN.

"I BELIEVE...I BELIEVE"

"The LORD is my shepherd, I shall not be in want. He makes me lie down in green pastures, he leads me beside quiet waters, he restores my soul. He guides me in paths of righteousness for his name's sake. Even though I walk through the valley of the shadow of death, I will fear no evil, for you are with me; your rod and your staff, they comfort me. You prepare a table before me in the presence of my enemies. You anoint my head with oil; my cup overflows. Surely goodness and love will follow me all the days of my life, and I will dwell in the house of the LORD forever."

Psalm 23:1–6

We move on now to ask yet another important question: Is God enough when grief over the loss of a loved one casts a dark shadow over our life? Grief comes to us all at one time or another. It is part of our earthly life, and from it none can escape. One poet worded it like this:

My son, the world is dark with grief and graves,
so dark that men cry out against the heavens.

It is likely that many of you reading these lines will be experiencing this type of sadness right now. Be assured, God knows how you feel. But more—His all-sufficient grace and power will support you at this difficult time.

Crying Out for Comfort

I once lived in a small town in the north of England, next door to a well-known businessman. He seemed as hard as nails. It was said that most of his staff quailed when he approached. Yet when his wife died and he knocked at my door, I was quite amazed at the difference I saw in him. This unfeeling man was distraught, and he cried out for comfort. "My business partners can't help me," he sobbed, "and my friends can't help me. You are a minister—can you help me?" I invited him in and listened as he poured out his grief. I told him that God could give him far more comfort than anyone else. I outlined for him the way of salvation, and he accepted Christ. Then this tough business-man went to my study window, looked up to heaven, and with tears coursing down his cheeks cried out three times: "I believe . . . I believe . . . I believe."

I tell you, when the hour comes in which we lose a person we love, no greater comfort can be found than the comfort God gives.

O merciful Father, Your heart, too, has known grief—grief over the death of Your own Son. And You still know grief, for all our griefs are Yours. Help me share my grief with You and thus halve it. In Christ's Name I pray. Amen.

GOD KNOWS HOW YOU FEEL.

THE FRIEND OF

FRIENDS

"The tongue has the power of life and death, and those who love it will eat its fruit. He who finds a wife finds what is good and receives favor from the LORD. A poor man pleads for mercy, but a rich man answers harshly. *A man of many companions may come to ruin, but there is a friend who sticks closer than a brother.*"

Proverbs 18:21–24

Who can mend a heart torn by grief and broken by the loss of a loved one? With all the conviction of which I am capable (and I speak from experience), I say, God can.

If we leave God out of the picture, what other sources of comfort are there? First and foremost, *friends.* Thank God for friends. Talking out one's grief with a close friend is a wonderful panacea for a grieving heart. I am grateful to the many friends who strengthened and supported me in the days following my wife's death, but as it has been said: "The best of friends are only friends at best." They can listen, they can sympathize, they can bring a sense of comfort and relief, but they are not an endless source of comfort in themselves. This is not said to devalue the power of friendship or deny that God can use it to soothe a torn heart. Over and over again when attempting to console someone who is grief stricken, I have heard the comment: "My friends have been such a comfort to me, but there is still a big hole in my life." My belief is that the Almighty God, the great *El-Shaddai,* can reach that hole and fill it. And I say once again: let no one think I am underestimating the power of friendship. It is a delightful supplement, but it can never be a substitute for the living God.

Comfort and Strength

Where can we find perfect comfort in the hour when the world has suddenly gone grey? What power can reach through the gloom without taking away the pain one needs to go through to complete the grieving process? Who can provide the inner strength that enables one to enter into life once again? Who is able? The great *El-Shaddai* is able. None better.

Father, while I am grateful for the comfort of friends, I realize that none can comfort the grieving heart like You. Your strength and enabling is available to me twenty-four hours of every day. Help me appropriate it. In Jesus' Name. Amen.

THANK GOD FOR FRIENDS.

INEFFECTUAL BEAUTY

"But now, this is what the LORD says—he who created you, O Jacob, he who formed you, O Israel: 'Fear not, for I have redeemed you; I have summoned you by name; you are mine. *When you pass through the waters, I will be with you;* and when you pass through the rivers, they will not sweep over you. When you walk through the fire, you will not be burned; the flames will not set you ablaze. For I am the LORD, your God, the Holy One of Israel, your Savior; I give Egypt for your ransom, Cush and Seba in your stead. Since you are precious and honored in my sight, and because I love you, I will give men in exchange for you, and people in exchange for your life. Do not be afraid, for I am with you.'"

Isaiah 43:1–5a

We continue thinking about some of the alternative sources of comfort people turn to when they are overcome with grief. Some turn to the arts. They seek comfort in music or pictures or sculpture.

Many years ago I took some American friends to the British Museum. In one of the art galleries we met a young woman who was crying. Sensitive inquiry informed us that she had just attended her mother's funeral and had come to the museum to try to find comfort amid the works of art and paintings. "Are they doing that for you?" asked one of my companions. "Not really," she replied. We told her about the comfort of God and the power of the great *El-Shaddai* (not using that term of course). Then we prayed with her. After we had done so, she dried her tears and told us that already God's comfort had started to help her.

Perfect Comfort

The arts can be a welcome aid when we are weighed down by grief, but like friendship, they can only supplement and never be a substitute for the comfort that God alone can give. Heinrich Heine, the exiled nineteenth-century German poet, loved all things beautiful. However, he discovered how limited is their power to heal when one day he knelt in tears before the Venus de Milo. Holding out his hands to the serene torso, he cried: "It is beautiful, but it has no arms." Art has no arms to lift one up in life's most bitter hour. A magnificent painting can seem like a sublime irrelevance; an exquisite statue, a thing of chilling beauty. Where is perfect comfort to be found? In God. The great *El-Shaddai* provides a comfort that reaches deep into the soul. No one can heal the hurts of the soul like the Almighty. He saves and succors and cares.

Thank You, my Father, that Your comfort and strength is mine for the asking. Though there are many beautiful things in the world from which I can draw some comfort, none is as beautiful as You.
Thank You, my Father. Amen.

NO ONE CAN HEAL THE HURTS OF THE
SOUL LIKE THE ALMIGHTY.

A L L A R E

S U P P L E M E N T S

"All this I have spoken while still with you. But the Counselor, the Holy Spirit, whom the Father will send in my name, will teach you all things and will remind you of everything I have said to you. *Peace I leave with you; my peace I give you.* I do not give to you as the world gives. Do not let your hearts be troubled and do not be afraid. You heard me say, 'I am going away and I am coming back to you.' If you loved me, you would be glad that I am going to the Father, for the Father is greater than I. I have told you now before it happens, so that when it does happen you will believe. I will not speak with you much longer, for the prince of this world is coming."

John 14:25–30a

What are some of the other routes people go down when seeking comfort for their grief? A number of people attempt to lose themselves in nature, and there is no doubt that the contemplation of majestic scenery does bring a measure of consolation.

Lord Avebury, in his book *The Marvels of the Universe*, said: "Nature will do much to soothe, comfort and console the troubled sorrows of life." His two-volume work of natural history helps us understand all about the polycystins and the foraminifera, extends our knowledge of the dinosaur and the diplodocus, but it is hard to find comfort in these things when our heart is heavy because we are mourning someone we love. Can we be blamed if we turn elsewhere? Ah, he would say, forget then the study of extinct creatures. Focus on the sweeping landscape, the majestic mountains, the loveliness of the hills and vales and trees and flowers. But again, these are all supplements. They help but they do not heal.

Respite or Real Comfort

What about good literature? Some advocate this when the heart is full of sorrow. I love literature, but I must admit that for all my love of books and my deep indebtedness to them in the hour of grief, the comfort they provide is inadequate. Books cannot really solace the desolate soul. Like nature they can help, but they cannot cure. You look at them and they seem strangely remote. They fail to reach the depths of your sorrow. Though they give some respite from mourning, you realize they cannot give enough. For the real source of comfort we must look elsewhere. But we don't have to look far. God in Christ offers us the kind of comfort for which there is no substitute.

My Father and my God, thank You for the comfort that You have vouchsafed to me through Your Son. When my heart throbs with pain, the peace He promised is not just an analgesic but brings, in time, a perfect cure. I am deeply grateful. Amen.

THEY HELP BUT THEY DO NOT HEAL.

TOUCHED WITH
OUR FEELINGS

"Therefore, since we have a great high priest who has gone through the heavens, Jesus the Son of God, let us hold firmly to the faith we profess. *For we do not have a high priest who is unable to sympathize with our weaknesses*, but we have one who has been tempted in every way, just as we are—yet was without sin. Let us then approach the throne of grace with confidence, so that we may receive mercy and grace to help us in our time of need."

Hebrews 4:14–16

If, as we have been saying, God alone perfectly restores the soul and gives us the comfort we need in our time of grief, how does He do this? He comes to people at such a time and gives their wounded spirits an awareness of His nearness and love that is more than enough to ease their sense of loss.

Emotional Pain

Note I use the word *ease*, not *eliminate.* Experiencing a sense of loss and staying with it until the grieving process is over is a necessary part of healing. Some therapists become alarmed at the existence of emotional pain and do their utmost to eliminate it. Our medical doctors act as quickly as they can to prevent us suffering physical pain—an action for which we are all grateful.

But emotional pain is quite different from physical pain. Undergoing the pain of grief contributes to the healing process, and the work of the great *El-Shaddai* is not to take it away but to help us bear it. The pain of grief is assuaged in time, but it is important that it does not go until the grief process has been worked through.

How long does that take? It varies, but in my own personal experience, and that of others with whom I have talked, it can last between six months and a year—sometimes longer. This length of time should not alarm you, especially if you are a Christian. It is during this period that God does His greatest work. He has felt grief through the experience of His own Son, the second Person of the Trinity, and knows what it is to suffer the same sorrow. Just think of it: Jesus has worn our flesh, measured its frailty, and knows exactly how we feel.

Father, I see that Your ministry to me in a time of grief is not to eliminate pain but to ease it. Your presence enables me to bear anything. A grief shared is a grief halved. I am truly grateful that I have One so great to share my grief. Amen.

EMOTIONAL PAIN IS QUITE DIFFERENT FROM PHYSICAL PAIN.

EXCESSIVE GRIEF

"When the Jews who had been with Mary in the house, comforting her, noticed how quickly she got up and went out, they followed her, supposing she was going to the tomb to mourn there. When Mary reached the place where Jesus was and saw him, she fell at his feet and said, 'Lord, if you had been here, my brother would not have died.' When Jesus saw her weeping, and the Jews who had come along with her also weeping, he was deeply moved in spirit and troubled. 'Where have you laid him?' he asked. 'Come and see, Lord,' they replied. *Jesus wept.* Then the Jews said, 'See how he loved him!'"

John 11:31–36

Since bereavement comes to us all at one time or another, we must ensure that when we do mourn we are not tipped into excessive grief. It isn't wrong to grieve. Today's text shows that Jesus Himself wept at the tomb of His dear friend Lazarus. Some Christians claim that if we are sure the person we loved has gone to heaven, then there is no need to grieve. I do not share that view. To suppress grief is psychologically and spiritually unproductive.

The apostle Paul said: "We do not want you to . . . grieve like the rest of men, who have no hope" (1 Thess. 4:13). Paul did not say that we should not grieve rather that we must not grieve like those without hope. He was a man of integrity, and he knew that even when we lose a loved one whom we know is in heaven, there will still be sorrow over the parting.

Denial of this can lead to problems. Some mourn to such a degree that they get sucked down into excessive grief— grief that continues for years.

Working Through Grief

To avoid excessive grief several things need to be done. First, accept the fact that the person you loved so dearly has gone, never to return to this world. This is the bitter part, but God is there to help you face reality. Next, avoid the temptation to suppress your grief and pretend that you are beyond such an emotional state. Cry when you feel like crying, even if you prefer to do it privately. Surrender yourself into the hands of God and invite Him to pour into you His grace and power. Then you will find that the blank wall of grief has a little open door through which you can walk into life again. God can help you get through grief. After all, He is, as we have been saying, "the Enough."

Father, whenever I experience grief, help me to deal with it in a way that cleanses and heals me without tipping over into excess. I remind myself once again that You are "the Enough." Amen.

GOD CAN HELP YOU GET THROUGH GRIEF.

Stars may be seen from the
bottom of a deep well when they
cannot be discerned from the top
of a mountain: so are many things
learned in adversity which the
prosperous dream not of. We need
affliction as the trees need winter
that we may collect sap and
nourishment for future blossoms
and fruit. Sorrow is as necessary for
the soul as medicine is for the body.

—Charles Haddon Spurgeon

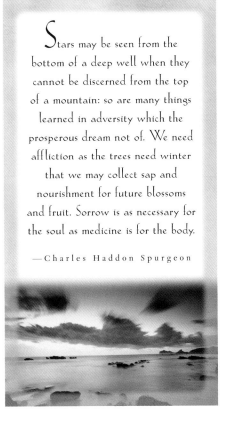

GOD The Enough

_____

_____

_____

_____

_____

_____

_____

_____

_____

_____

_____

_____

_____

_____

_____

_____

_____

_____

_____

_____

_____

_____

Journal Entry

KINDS OF TRIAL

I see his blood upon the rose,
And in the stars the glory
of his eyes,
His body gleams amid the
eternal snows,
His tears drop from the skies.
All pathways by his feet are worn,
His strong heart stirs the
everbeating sea,
His crown of thorns is twined
with every thorn,
His cross is every tree.

— E.M. Plunkett

"TO THE TUNE OF 'SUFFERING'"

"But we have this treasure in jars of clay to show that this all-surpassing power is from God and not from us. *We are hard pressed on every side, but not crushed*; perplexed, but not in despair; persecuted, but not abandoned; *struck down, but not destroyed.* We always carry around in our body the death of Jesus, so that the life of Jesus may also be revealed in our body. For we who are alive are always being given over to death for Jesus' sake, so that his life may be revealed in our mortal body. So then, death is at work in us, but life is at work in you."

2 Corinthians 4:7–12

The next question we reflect on is this: Is God enough when we are worn down as a result of long-term sickness and suffering? While I was leafing through the Moffatt translation of the Bible, I was intrigued by the heading to Psalm 53, which reads: "From the choirmaster's collection: to the tune of 'Suffering.'" No doubt many reading these lines today are living out their lives to the tune of suffering. This is the dominant note. Is the great *El-Shaddai* able to succor us when we are weary with sickness and suffering—when every known resource of healing seems ineffective? I dare to believe He can.

I am increasingly convinced of the truth of Oswald Chambers' words that I have often quoted: "Life is more tragic than orderly." It seems almost every other person I speak to has experienced severe suffering. Take these situations that were brought to my attention in visits overseas. In Uganda, I once preached in a church with over six thousand people in its congregation. Almost every family in the church, I was informed, was in some way affected by the deadful disease of AIDS. In Kenya, a fine Christian couple told me that their first child had just been born but was seriously incapacitated. In Canada, a businessman sadly described how his twin daughters—just three years old—had contracted a disease that causes permanent blindness.

Answers?

In such situations it isn't easy to come up with answers. There are answers—intellectual ones. However, God gives us something better than answers. He gives us a richer sense of His presence. He gives us *Himself*. Answers satisfy the intellect; the presence of the great *El-Shaddai* satisfies the soul.

Gracious and loving heavenly Father,
how thankful I am that when suffering comes Your
presence is enough to hold and carry me through.
Thank You, my Father. In Jesus' Name. Amen.

"LIFE IS MORE TRAGIC THAN ORDERLY."

P O W E R —

A L L - S U R P A S S I N G

"To keep me from becoming conceited because of these surpassingly great revelations, there was given me a thorn in my flesh, a messenger of Satan, to torment me. Three times I pleaded with the Lord to take it away from me. But he said to me, *'My grace is sufficient for you, for my power is made perfect in weakness.'* Therefore I will boast all the more gladly about my weaknesses, so that Christ's power may rest on me. That is why, for Christ's sake, I delight in weaknesses, in insults, in hardships, in persecutions, in difficulties. For when I am weak, then I am strong."

2 Corinthians 12:7–10

We continue reflecting on the fact that many live out their lives to the tune of suffering. Sir Arthur Conan Doyle once described what made him a materialist early in life. It is a moving story. As a physician, he constantly saw sights that he could not reconcile with the idea of a merciful God. On one occasion he was called to a poor woman's home to attend to her daughter. When he entered the humble dwelling, he saw a cot on one side of the room and, following the mother's gesture, made his way to it. He bent over, expecting to find a child. What he saw was a pair of brown sullen eyes full of loathing and pain that looked up at him in resentment. He could not tell how old the creature was. Long thin limbs were twisted and coiled on the tiny cot. The face was sane but malignant. "What is it?" he asked in dismay after taking it all in. "It's a girl," sobbed the mother. "She's nineteen. Oh, if only God would take her."

Sickness and Disease

Some types of illness (even in this modern age when medical knowledge is so advanced) are proof against every form of cure. Disease takes its dreadful course, and often all that can be done is to alleviate the pain. We know that sickness is the direct result of Adam and Eve's sin, and we know, too, that in heaven all suffering will be banished. We accept also that God can and does heal. Indeed, we must never lose sight of that glorious fact. But if He doesn't, what then? He provides the strength for us to get through every day. We, too, can experience what Paul describes in our passage today: the all-surpassing power of God. Either way we win.

Father, I see that when I cry for deliverance from sickness and suffering and for some reason release doesn't come, I am not bereft of Your power and Your strength. Although Your power does not necessarily deliver me from it, Your power will always carry me through. Amen.

GOD PROVIDES THE STRENGTH FOR
US TO GET THROUGH EVERY DAY.

I L L N E S S —

M A D E   T O   W O R K

"I plead with you, brothers, become like me, for I became like you. You have done me no wrong. *As you know, it was because of an illness that I first preached the gospel to you.* Even though my illness was a trial to you, you did not treat me with contempt or scorn. Instead, you welcomed me as if I were an angel of God, as if I were Christ Jesus himself. What has happened to all your joy? I can testify that, if you could have done so, you would have torn out your eyes and given them to me. Have I now become your enemy by telling you the truth?"

Galatians 4:12–16

In the past, after I have written on the subject of sickness and suffering, a number of readers have taken me to task for not making more of the fact that God heals. There is no doubt in my mind that miraculous healing does take place in answer to prayer—no doubt whatsoever. On many occasions in my life I have experienced direct healing from God. When I was thirty I was struck down with an illness that puzzled my doctors, and I was given three days to live. God came to me through the words of John 10:10 (KJV): "I am come that they might have life, and that they might have it more abundantly." Miraculously, He healed me. My belief in divine healing is unimpeachable.

Healing Or Not

But God does not always heal. Why, we cannot fully understand. Some Christians are convinced that God is willing to heal every illness and that if healing does not come then the fault lies with us: we do not have enough faith; some secret sin remains unconfessed; something in our family's history may be blocking the healing; we do not really want to be healed; and so on. In some instances one of these matters may well be the case and, when seeking healing, it is helpful to look at the factors mentioned. The confession of sin, for example, is clearly tied to healing, as can be seen from James 5:16.

There are times, however, when God will not heal an illness because He sees a better purpose can be achieved through it than through healing. Look at our text for today once again. It was because of an illness, Paul says, that he preached the Gospel to the Galatians. Limited by ill health, he stayed where he was, raised up a church, and afterwards wrote a letter to it that has enriched the world.

O Father, I rejoice that You can take everything and turn it to advantage—even illness. You make everything sing—suffering included. This adds a new dimension to life. I am so grateful. Amen.

GOD DOES NOT ALWAYS HEAL.

E N O U G H —
F O R E V E R M O R E

"Praise be to the God and Father of our Lord Jesus Christ! In his great mercy he has given us new birth into a living hope through the resurrection of Jesus Christ from the dead, and into an inheritance that can never perish, spoil or fade— kept in heaven for you, who through faith are shielded by God's power until the coming of the salvation that is ready to be revealed in the last time. In this you *greatly rejoice, though now for a little while you may have had to suffer grief in all kinds of trials.* These have come so that your faith—of greater worth than gold, which perishes even though refined by fire— may be proved genuine and may result in praise, glory and honor when Jesus Christ is revealed."

1 Peter 1:3–7

A balanced view of the subject of healing holds in tension the fact that God does heal but that there are times when He allows sickness to continue because a greater purpose can be achieved through it than through healing. Some of the most notable Christians have had to struggle with disability or infirmity.

Saints Who Suffered

Not long ago I went through my library making a list of the illustrious saints in church history who struggled with poor health. I was astonished. The list seemed endless. There was Teresa of Avila who recorded that she was in constant, though cheerful, conflict with ill health, battling with terrible headaches which she described as "those rushing waterfalls in my head." She also suffered several bouts of chronic fever and at least one stroke that partially paralyzed her. There was Henry Martyn, the missionary to India, who struggled with tuberculosis; Francis Chavisse, a French missionary to Africa, who was meekly resigned to his humpback; and the blind George Matheson, who thanked God for his thorn. Nor should we forget Catherine Booth of the Salvation Army, who endured years of pain that she would never permit to be dulled. And this is to name but a few.

But there are countless modern spiritual heroes too—people like those of you reading these words who are enduring sickness and pain yet still clinging to God and rejoicing in the sufficiency of His grace. In triumph you sing:

Its streams the whole creation reach,
So plenteous is its store;
Enough for all, enough for each,
Enough for evermore.

O Father, it's almost unthinkable that You could ever leave me without sufficient grace to face whatever comes my way. I am glad I do not even have to face the possibility. You are enough—more than enough for everything. And enough forevermore. Amen.

SOME OF THE MOST NOTABLE CHRISTIANS HAVE HAD
TO STRUGGLE WITH DISABILITY OR INFIRMITY.

A STRANGE INTERTWINING

"Praise be to the God and Father of our Lord Jesus Christ, the Father of compassion and the God of all comfort, *who comforts us in all our troubles, so that we can comfort those in any trouble* with the comfort we ourselves have received from God. For just as the sufferings of Christ flow over into our lives, so also through Christ our comfort overflows. If we are distressed, it is for your comfort and salvation; if we are comforted, it is for your comfort, which produces in you patient endurance of the same sufferings we suffer. And our hope for you is firm, because we know that just as you share in our sufferings, so also you share in our comfort."

2 Corinthians 1:3–7

The path of pain and suffering is a dark one, and we are grateful for every beam of light that shines across it. One ray of light I have discovered is this: in some mysterious way, joy and pain intertwine. They are not really opposites; they belong together. Some argue that they are irreconcilable and contrast one with the other, but I believe that notion to be false. They often go hand in hand. In joy are babies conceived (except, of course, in the case of rape), but in pain and labor are they brought into the world. This amazing thing that we call "mother-love" is woven in woe.

Sympathy

I see, too, that pain and suffering render a rich service to the human race. The most deeply sympathetic are those who have suffered most profoundly. Often in those who have not experienced some degree of suffering, sympathy is a shallow stream. And sympathy is far too precious for us to cavil at the price that must be paid to procure it. When the Puritan Richard Baxter lost his wife, he became grief-stricken and said: "I will not be judged by any that has not felt the like." It was his way of saying that he could not be comforted by anyone who had not suffered in a similar way. A Christian's suffering can be wrested into service. It is Christlike work to soothe and sympathize, and only those who have drunk the cup of suffering are fully equipped to do it.

So I ask the question again: Is God enough when we are called to endure illness and suffering, when we ask for healing but it does not come? Those who know Him and have experienced His unfailing grace will say without equivocation that He is. They do what the oyster does with its pain. They turn it into a pearl.

Father, I am deeply grateful that by Your grace things can be transformed, even suffering and sickness. The comfort You give me can be used to comfort others. Thank You, my Father. Amen.

SUFFERING RENDERS A RICH SERVICE TO THE HUMAN RACE.

Nothing Unknown To Him

"O LORD, you have searched me and you know me. You know when I sit and when I rise; you perceive my thoughts from afar. You discern my going out and my lying down; you are familiar with all my ways. Before a word is on my tongue you know it completely, O LORD. You hem me in—behind and before; you have laid your hand upon me. Such knowledge is too wonderful for me, too lofty for me to attain. Where can I go from your Spirit? Where can I flee from your presence? If I go up to the heavens, you are there; if I make my bed in the depths, you are there. If I rise on the wings of the dawn, if I settle on the far side of the sea, even there your hand will guide me, your right hand will hold me fast."

Psalm 139:1–10

Over the past weeks we have considered a number of areas where we have seen that God can prove He is enough. Now we come to the issue of secret sorrows—those bitter griefs and memories that are thought about or sobbed out in secret. Can God be enough here?

Secrets

Some of the worst sorrows the human heart can harbor are *secret* sorrows. I have learned this from the confidences shared with me during hundreds of hours in the counseling room.

People have unfolded things to me—secret troubles and sadnesses—that they have not shared with another human being. Needless to say, these confidences are locked in my heart and will go with me to the grave. Yet many people do not have the opportunity (or desire) to share with a counselor or close friend the secrets they hide in their hearts. In some cases the nature of the secret makes it difficult or impossible to share with another. Then there are some who would like to share a secret sorrow but feel it wrong to impose their pain on another person. We Britishers are renowned for this. Our upbringing has taught us to restrain our expressions of sorrow. We call it maintaining a stiff upper lip. One British writer says: "It does not belong to the nature of our people to make a pageant of a bleeding heart."

Sharing our secret burdens with a confidant can be helpful, but what if the nature of the problem or the lack of a confidant makes that impossible? Is God enough then? I believe He is. Though it is good to have a human ear into which to pour our troubles and a human face to reflect our pain, it is not absolutely necessary. Prayer brings God close—closer than the dearest friend.

My Lord and my God, I am thankful there is nothing I cannot share with You. My secret sorrows are known to You. Forgive me that I share the secret things on my heart so infrequently with You. Help me to be more communicative. In Jesus' Name. Amen.

PRAYER BRINGS GOD CLOSE.

COMFORT — NOT
CELEBRATE

"The very fact that you have lawsuits among you means that you have been completely defeated already. Why not rather be wronged? Why not rather be cheated? Instead, you yourselves cheat and do wrong, and you do this to your brothers. Do you not know that the wicked will not inherit the kingdom of God? Do not be deceived: Neither the sexually immoral nor idolaters nor adulterers nor male prostitutes nor homosexual offenders nor thieves nor the greedy nor drunkards nor slanderers nor swindlers will inherit the kingdom of God. *And that is what some of you were.* But you were washed, you were sanctified, you were justified in the name of the Lord Jesus Christ and by the Spirit of our God."

1 Corinthians 6:7–11

We said yesterday that often the human heart harbors *secret* sorrows. Frequently men and women walk about with a brave smile on their faces while inwardly they are bearing the pain of a lacerated heart. Take, for example, the issue of homosexual inclinations. There will be some reading these lines today who find themselves attracted to members of the same sex. They do not intend to act on those feelings, but because of the homophobia in certain parts of the church, many are afraid to share how they feel. They carry a secret sorrow.

Homosexual Inclinations

Now let me make it clear that, like most evangelicals, I differentiate between homosexual inclinations and homosexual practice. Scripture leads me to conclude that it is homosexual practice, not homosexual feelings, that God condemns (see Lev. 20:13). And those who say God has made some with an affection for their own sex are showing their ignorance of Scripture. Homosexual inclination, as John Stott puts it, "is not a sign of a created order, but a sign of a fallen disorder." Sin has tampered with our nature, and we should not celebrate our fallenness but confront it in the power and grace given to us by Jesus Christ.

Just as believers who are heterosexual have to draw on God's resources when tempted by the opposite sex, so those who are homosexually inclined should do the same. Any man or woman struggling with the secret sorrow of homosexual inclinations can come in confidence to God. He gives us the strength to combat temptation and can bring about great changes in the personality also. He did so in the first century—why not in this? Listen to Paul's words once again: "And that is what some of you *were*."

Father, I see that Your creation that was made perfect has gone astray through sin. Help me understand this, for without this key I will never be able to understand the complexities of human behavior. In Jesus' Name I pray. Amen.

GOD GIVES US THE STRENGTH TO COMBAT TEMPTATION.

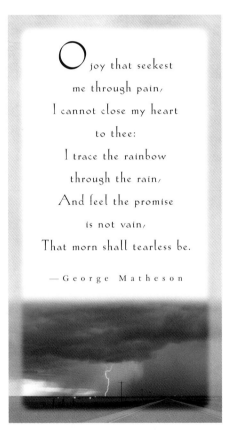

O joy that seekest

me through pain,

I cannot close my heart

to thee:

I trace the rainbow

through the rain,

And feel the promise

is not vain,

That morn shall tearless be.

—George Matheson

GOD The Enough

_____

_____

_____

_____

_____

_____

_____

_____

_____

_____

_____

_____

_____

_____

_____

_____

_____

_____

_____

_____

_____

_____

_____

_____

_____

_____

_____

_____

_____

_____

_____

_____

_____

_____

_____

_____

_____

_____

_____

_____

SUSTAINED
BY
GOD'S LOVE

And now in age I bud again;

After so many deaths I live.

— George Herbert

S C A R R E D
M E M O R I E S

"Here is my servant, whom I uphold, my chosen one in whom I delight; I will put my Spirit on him and he will bring justice to the nations. He will not shout or cry out, or raise his voice in the streets. *A bruised reed he will not break, and a smoldering wick he will not snuff out.* In faithfulness he will bring forth justice; he will not falter or be discouraged till he establishes justice on earth."

Isaiah 42:1–4a

Secret sorrows are, of course, of all sorts. For one woman I know, a deaconess, it is this: her father was a murderer. The crime was committed in a different part of the country—she and her family moved to where they now live to make a fresh start. "I am afraid to tell anyone about this," she confided, "because of the possible rejection my family and I might suffer if the facts were made known." She carried a secret sorrow.

Secret Sadness

For others the secret sadness might be the poignant remembrance of some youthful folly, the burning recollection of a harvest of wild oats, a misdeed that has scarred the memory. A minister I have met, well known and highly respected in the country where he preaches, told me of an occasion in his youth when he was part of a group who raped a young woman. "I know God has forgiven me for this," he said, "but there is hardly a day when my mind does not go back to it. It is all past and gone and of course forgiven, but I carry a sorrow that I don't think will ever leave." The range of secret sorrows is so varied: there is the corroding care of a business that is not successful and is hardly likely to be; the suspicion that a husband or wife is being unfaithful though there is no proof; the fear that the mental illness suffered by a parent will be inherited; regrets concerning one's dealings with a person who has since died and to whom one cannot say "sorry"; the shame of having been sexually abused by one's father.

Can God sustain the heart that carries such secret sorrows? Without doubt He can. His grace not only brings about forgiveness for our sin but continues its work when our hearts are weighed down with private burdens.

O Father, Your forgiveness and healing removes the acuteness of painful memories, but sorrow sometimes continues to reside in the heart. How glad I am that Your grace is enough to support me even in this. Thank You, my Father. Amen.

GOD'S GRACE BRINGS ABOUT FORGIVENESS FOR OUR SIN.

U N E N V I A B L E
S U C C E S S

"Humble yourselves, therefore, under God's mighty hand, that he may lift you up in due time. *Cast all your anxiety on him because he cares for you.* Be self-controlled and alert. Your enemy the devil prowls around like a roaring lion looking for someone to devour. Resist him, standing firm in your faith, because you know that your brothers throughout the world are undergoing the same kind of sufferings. And the God of all grace, who called you to his eternal glory in Christ, after you have suffered a little while, will himself restore you and make you strong, firm and steadfast. To him be the power for ever and ever. Amen."

1 Peter 5:6–11

Biography is full of illustrations of hidden griefs. At school I had to study the life of Charles V, emperor of Germany and king of Spain, in order to write an essay. I found him to be one of the most interesting men of history. He had a large share of what we would term "success," and at the height of his power (the mid-sixteenth century), his personality dominated Europe. Yet he carried a secret sorrow. He never felt satisfied with what life had given him; inwardly he longed for a simpler, less complicated life. No one knew of his secret longing until one day, in 1556, he threw aside not one but half a dozen crowns and gave up the life he had lived in order to enter a monastery. He was a man who was all-powerful, but all miserable. The pomp and trappings of monarchy hid a heavy heart. He told a friend: "I was forced into a life that really I never wanted, and now I have all that my heart has ever longed for—solitude. Now I am content." This is why envy is so misplaced.

Appearances May Deceive

In one church I pastored there was a man who was far richer than the other members. One day one of the poorer members of the congregation, referring to the man with a great deal of money, said: "How I envy him. He has everything one could want. I wish I could change places with him." But he saw only the surface of things. I happened to know that a secret sorrow saddened the life of that man. He was suffering from a painful and incurable disease that he had told no one else about.

When you look at people who seem to have everything, don't envy them and long to change places with them. Success is not always what it seems.

Father, psychologists tell us that inward bruises are sometimes the worst bruises. They give no outward sign; no discoloration is observable to the eye. Yet all is open to You. You see deep into the heart and are swift to strengthen and support. I am so grateful. Amen.

SUCCESS IS NOT ALWAYS WHAT IT SEEMS.

"A S I L E N T S O B"

"As the king of Israel was passing by on the wall, a woman cried to him, 'Help me, my lord the king!' The king replied, 'If the LORD does not help you, where can I get help for you? From the threshing floor? From the winepress?' Then he asked her, 'What's the matter?' She answered, 'This woman said to me, "Give up your son so we may eat him today, and tomorrow we'll eat my son." So we cooked my son and ate him. The next day I said to her, "Give up your son so we may eat him," but she had hidden him.' When the king heard the woman's words, he tore his robes. As he went along the wall, *the people looked, and there, underneath, he had sackcloth on his body.*"

2 Kings 6:26–30

Today we look at a biblical character who illustrates perhaps better than anyone else in the Old Testament the point I am making about secret sorrows. His name is King Jehoram.

Siege Conditions

Samaria is under siege, and the people have nothing to eat. A donkey's head, we are told, sold for eighty shekels (about two pounds) of silver! King Jehoram walks among his people, presumably in order to encourage and inspire them. As he passes by, a woman shouts out: "Help me, my lord the king." The king stops to listen. Pointing to a woman standing nearby, she complains: "This woman said to me, 'Give up your son so we may eat him today, and tomorrow we'll eat my son.' So we cooked my son and ate him. The next day I said to her, 'Give up your son so that we may eat him,' but she had hidden him" (vv. 28–29). The king is so upset by what he hears that he tears his robes—the recognized expression of grief. As he continues on his way, the people notice that underneath his torn robes, next to his skin, he is wearing sackcloth.

Sackcloth, as you know, is extremely coarse fabric. The king was dressed in his royal garments as he mingled with the people, but beneath them, next to his skin, was sackcloth. It was a symbol of heartbreak—a silent sob. He wore it where it would be hidden, not as an outer garment that everyone could see. Outside he looked fine, but inside his heart was breaking, and the sackcloth symbolized his grief. The highway of hurt is a crowded highway. A poet put it well when he said:

For if every man's eternal care were written on his brow,
How many would our pity share who have our envy now?

Father, I wonder how many I will meet today who secretly are wearing sackcloth. The world is filled with sadness. Help me in the future to walk more sensitively, bearing in mind that people may be hurting more than I realize. In Jesus' Name I pray. Amen.

THE HIGHWAY OF HURT IS A CROWDED HIGHWAY.

"No One But You, Lord!"

"Keep me safe, O God, for in you I take refuge. I said to the LORD, *'You are my Lord; apart from you I have no good thing.'* As for the saints who are in the land, they are the glorious ones in whom is all my delight. The sorrows of those will increase who run after other gods. I will not pour out their libations of blood or take up their names on my lips. LORD, you have assigned me my portion and my cup; you have made my lot secure. The boundary lines have fallen for me in pleasant places; surely I have a delightful inheritance. I will praise the LORD, who counsels me; even at night my heart instructs me. I have set the LORD always before me. Because he is at my right hand, I will not be shaken."

Psalm 16:1–8

We return to the question we posed a few days ago: Is God enough when our hearts are lacerated by secret sorrows? I hope I have made a strong case for the fact that He is. Many times I have sat in a counseling room and listened as people have shared their secret sorrows with me—matters they have never revealed to another human being. It is a privilege to be trusted with such confidences, and, as I have said, I would no more dream of breaking them than I would of injuring one of my children.

Trusting

It is always gratifying to see how the sharing of some secret sorrow brings relief. One woman said: "If you only had some idea what it means to me to know that at least one other being is now aware of this." I was reminded of what Sydney Jourard said in his book *The Transparent Self*, a helpful secular book: "Every one of us longs to get alongside someone before we die and say, 'Let me share with you my deepest secrets.'" But whom can we trust to share our deepest secrets or sorrows? Not many, I am afraid. My reply to the woman's comment was: "The relief it has brought you to share a secret sorrow with me is obvious, but tell me—if you had not found someone with whom you could share it, would you have still been able to go on, realizing that only God knew?" What I was asking was this: Is God enough? She thought and then replied: "Yes, I would have been able to go on. It has helped to share this matter with someone, but if I had not had that privilege, I could still have carried on, drawing on His all-sufficient grace."

That is the testimony of countless thousands who, having no one else to share their secret sorrows with, find that in such situations God proves Himself "the Enough."

Father, the conviction is growing stronger day
by day that no matter what situation in which
I find myself, You are "the Enough." I can do
without many things, but I cannot do without You.
Blessed be Your Name forever. Amen.

THE SHARING OF SOME SECRET SORROW BRINGS RELIEF.

PALMY DAYS

"The next day *the great crowd* that had come for the Feast *heard that Jesus was on his way to Jerusalem. They took palm branches* and went out to meet him, shouting, 'Hosanna!' 'Blessed is he who comes in the name of the Lord!' 'Blessed is the King of Israel!' Jesus found a young donkey and sat upon it, as it is written, 'Do not be afraid, O daughter of Zion; see, your king is coming, seated on a donkey's colt.' At first his disciples did not understand all this. Only after Jesus was glorified did they realize that these things had been written about him and that they had done these things to him."

John 12:12–16

We now ask the question: Is God enough when palmy days are past and gone? Perhaps the term "palmy days" is unfamiliar to you, so permit me to explain. The palm is a symbol of triumph. In countries where the tree flourishes, it was used as a sign of victory and conquest, and hence became a symbol of success. Thus, when speaking of a man or woman's days of outstanding accomplishment, we refer to them as their palmy days.

In the passage we have read today, we find that the Jews greeted Jesus on His entry into Jerusalem with palms. They were not waving palm branches because they were the most convenient things to grab hold of; they were doing so to acclaim Him, to register the fact He was highly regarded. This was, we might say, our Lord's palmy day. Some believe it was the most highly acclaimed hour of His life. But it did not last long. A week later He was on a cross! One day He was the object of adulation—a few days later, the object of shame. Life is like that. You can be honored one day and the next day cast aside as if you were nothing. Our Lord knew what it was to see a palmy day turn into a shadowy day. Yet He found His Father to be enough.

God Is Still God

For some of you, the palmy days—the days of outstanding success and achievement—may be a mere memory. But never forget that God is still God. The days may come and go, but He remains changeless. He is with you just as much now as He was then. Your name is written on the palm of His hands. Do you realize what that means? He can never look at the palm of His hands without thinking of you. Others may have forgotten you and your achievements, but you can never, never be forgotten by Him.

Father, what hope and encouragement it gives me to know that when palmy days are past, You are still "the Enough." Your grace exceeds all my require- ments, and Your resources are more than a match for my every need. Thank You, my Father. Amen.

GOD CAN NEVER LOOK AT THE PALM OF
HIS HANDS WITHOUT THINKING OF YOU.

"T H R E E   S C O R E   S U M M E R S"

"The righteous will flourish like a palm tree, they will grow like a cedar of Lebanon; planted in the house of the LORD, they will flourish in the courts of our God. *They will still bear fruit in old age*, they will stay fresh and green, *proclaiming, 'The LORD is upright*; He is my Rock, and there is no wickedness in him.'"

Psalm 92:12—15

Most people will have some experience of what we are calling palmy days. It is a poor sort of human life that has no palmy days at all. Perhaps I am talking at this moment to someone whose palmy days seem to have come and gone. Your mind lingers on the good times, the successful times, which now seem to be over or coming to a close. In my life I have been struck by many things, not the least its transience. How quickly the good times seem to be over.

We saw yesterday that our Lord experienced this. One day they shouted for Him; a few days later they crucified Him. One day palms, another day thorns. Could anything be more pitiable? Our Lord fell from favor so quickly that there seems to have been no in-between stage. One day He was hailed as a king; less than a week later He was denounced as a criminal. How typical of life.

Retirement Years

What is it like with you? Are the years catching up with you, and you feel the best of life has gone? You may have retired or be on the point of retiring, and the words of the poet describe your feelings:

Three score summers when they're gone
appear as short as one.

Don't, I beg you, lapse into self-pity. With God it need not be like that. It may be true that your energy is not as great as it used to be, but this makes no difference to the quality of the life that God has given you. He can hold you and impart His strength and power to you in the most amazing way. He is "the Enough" not only in youth or middle age but in the twilight years as well.

O Father, help me to grow old graciously, to come to maturity majestically. Fill my heart with the assurance that no matter what the future holds for me, You are ever and always "the Enough." In Christ's Name I pray. Amen.

DON'T LAPSE INTO SELF-PITY.

T H E   H I G H E R ,
T H E   C L E A R E R

"Listen to me, O house of Jacob, all you who remain of the house of Israel, you whom I have upheld since you were conceived, and have carried since your birth. *Even to your old age and gray hairs I am he,* I am he who will sustain you. *I have made you and I will carry you*; I will sustain you and I will rescue you. To whom will you compare me or count me equal? To whom will you liken me that we may be compared? Some pour out gold from their bags and weigh out silver on the scales; they hire a goldsmith to make it into a god, and they bow down and worship it."

Isaiah 46:3–6

We are reflecting on the question: Is God enough when the palmy days are past and gone? Though this question has relevance to every stage of life, it is of particular significance to those who find themselves in what we call "the advancing years." Now that I myself am at the stage of life known as the "pensionable period." I have a viewpoint that is more than theoretical. The other day I found myself feeling irritated when I opened a magazine and read this: "Old age comes to us all; the accent of the orator fails, the touch of the painter grows unsure, the voice of the singer weakens." All true of course, but so one-sided.

The Benefits of God

Permit me to present the other side of the picture. As you climb the steps of a tower, the horizons broaden, and the view becomes clearer and more extensive. This is how we should think of our view of life—the older we get, the more clearly we can see. People often say to me nowadays: "Wouldn't you like to be eighteen again?" I wouldn't be eighteen again for anything. Longfellow, the poet, put it like this:

How far the gulf stream of our youth may flow
Into the arctic region of our lives
For age is opportunity no less
Than youth itself, though in another dress,
And as the evening twilight fades away
The sky is filled with stars, invisible by day.

The closing years of life can be the best years of life. God is with you, and you have had a running start.

Father, I am determined that the years
will not creep up on me like a dreaded disease.
I shall meet them with cheer because I am ageless
in You. I have had a running start, and
I press on toward what lies ahead. Amen.

THE CLOSING YEARS OF LIFE CAN BE THE BEST YEARS OF LIFE.

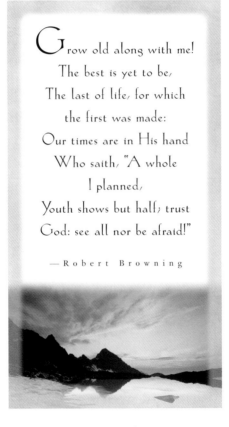

Grow old along with me!
The best is yet to be,
The last of life, for which
the first was made:
Our times are in His hand
Who saith, "A whole
I planned,
Youth shows but half; trust
God: see all nor be afraid!"

—Robert Browning

Journal Entry

DARKNESS IS AS LIGHT TO GOD

Those are perfect in faith who can come to God in the utter dearth of their feelings and desires—without a glow or an aspiration, with the weight of low thoughts, failures, neglect and wandering forgetfulness—and say to him, "Thou art my refuge."

— George MacDonald

NO CAMOUFLAGES

"For you have been my hope, O Sovereign LORD, my confidence since my youth. From birth I have relied on you; you brought me forth from my mother's womb. I will ever praise you. I have become like a portent to many, but you are my strong refuge. My mouth is filled with your praise, declaring your splendor all day long. *Do not cast me away when I am old; do not forsake me when my strength is gone.* For my enemies speak against me; those who wait to kill me conspire together. They say, 'God has forsaken him; pursue him and seize him, for no one will rescue him.' Be not far from me, O God; come quickly, O my God, to help me."

Psalm 71:5–12

"Aging can be beautiful," said E. Stanley Jones, "but to make it so we must bring to it something that makes it beautiful." The apostle Peter, writing to women, said: "Your beauty should not come from outward adornment . . . it should be that of your inner self, the unfading beauty of a gentle and quiet spirit" (1 Pet. 3:3–4). We bring what we have developed into old age. If we have developed a beautiful spirit, it will still be there when we grow old, and can be more beautiful still. In fact, it has been said: "We don't grow old; we get old by not growing." I came across this on an epitaph some years ago: "He was always growing." I hope that can be said of me too. How about you?

Forgive a personal reference again, but a lovely thing was said to me one day. A man who heard me speak at a meeting in Nairobi thirty years ago, and who had not seen me since, commented: "When I met you all those years ago, I saw the Welsh fire in your soul and wondered what would happen when you got older. Many speakers lose their fire over the years, but you have not. In fact, it seems you have more now than you had then." I don't mind telling you I came away feeling that if I'd had a hat I would have thrown it in the air!

Still Growing

If it is true that we don't grow old but get old by not growing, how do we keep on growing? Well, we can't keep from getting old by depending on camouflages—disguises such as dress and paint. How pathetic it is to see someone trying to hide their age by plastering their face with cosmetics. Age stares out from behind this unattractive coating. A little is fine, but a lot shouts: "I am not comfortable with growing old." Painting a dead tree with green paint doesn't make it living. Life is within.

Father, whatever the future holds for me, make my advanced years tender with love, strong with Your strength, and may I grow with Your life. This I ask in Christ's peerless and precious Name. Amen.

"WE DON'T GROW OLD; WE GET OLD BY NOT GROWING."

A Ladder For Old Age

"But as for me, I will always have hope; I will praise you more and more. My mouth will tell of your righteousness, of your salvation all day long, though I know not its measure. I will come and proclaim your mighty acts, O Sovereign LORD; I will proclaim your righteousness, yours alone. Since my youth, O God, you have taught me, and to this day I declare your marvelous deeds. *Even when I am old and gray, do not forsake me, O God, till I declare your power to the next generation*, your might to all who are to come. Your righteousness reaches to the skies, O God, you who have done great things. Who, O God, is like you? Though you have made me see troubles, many and bitter, you will restore my life again; from the depths of the earth you will again bring me up."

Psalm 71:14–20

The point being made in this section of our meditations is this: The touch of God's creative Spirit can be upon us, affecting both our activities and our character, right on into old age. Thank God growing old physically does not mean we stop growing spiritually. Let me give you a ladder on which to climb into old age.

Growing Spiritually

First, *accept your age*. Don't fight the fact you are getting old—use it. You can't be twenty-five, so make sixty-five beautiful and useful. At sixty-five you can possess a calm and poise you did not have when you were twenty-five.

Second, *accept the responsibilities that come through new freedoms*. The children have grown up and gone—now see what you can do for other children. If you can't work to help children, then find some other sphere of activity into which you can pour your life's experience.

Third, *expunge the word* retirement *from your vocabulary*. Don't admit to being retired. Tell people you have changed your work. The retirement mentality is something that must be shed. You have been made for creativity, and that never stops. You may not create as energetically as before, but you can create. If you don't create, you will grow tired resting. Ask God to show you how you can use your experience to help others. Never, never, never stop being creative.

Fourth, *develop your mind, if you can, right up to the end*. Those, of course, who are affected by some form of dementia will not be able to do this, but nevertheless they can still worship and witness to God's grace. If no physical affliction prevents you, read a good book every week. Above all, fill your mind with *the* book—the Bible. Then you will never stop growing, never be empty, and never be alone.

Dear God, don't let me settle down. Prod me from within if this ever starts to happen. I am not as old as my arteries but as my attitudes. Let me die growing. I ask this in and through the precious Name of Jesus. Amen.

YOU HAVE BEEN MADE FOR CREATIVITY,
AND THAT NEVER STOPS.

"R O U N D   Y O U R

F A C E S"

"After this I looked and there before me was a great multitude that no one could count, from every nation, tribe, people and language, standing before the throne and in front of the Lamb. *They were wearing white robes and were holding palm branches in their hands.* And they cried out in a loud voice: 'Salvation belongs to our God, who sits on the throne, and to the Lamb.' All the angels were standing around the throne and around the elders and the four living creatures. They fell down on their faces before the throne and worshiped God, saying: 'Amen! Praise and glory and wisdom and thanks and honor and power and strength be to our God for ever and ever. Amen!'"

Revelation 7:9–12

Though the palmy days may be in the past, that does not mean good things cannot still be experienced and enjoyed. And I would argue that not all our greatest achievements belong to our palmy days. Many do their most effective work when the prime of life is past. Some research into which years are the most productive found that 64 percent of famous achievements have been accomplished by people over sixty.

The same was true in biblical times. Take Eli, for example. He might have thought his palmy days were over, but God gave him Samuel. Nothing that Eli ever did, in my opinion, was greater than his training and shaping of Samuel. The boy went on to become one of Israel's greatest prophets, and much of his success could be credited to Eli's influence and instruction.

Heaven

But let me conclude with this thought: it is only earth's palmy days that are behind us. The real palmy days are ahead. In the passage before us today, John sees a multitude that no one could number from every nation, tribe, people, and language. They were standing before the throne and the Lamb and were dressed in white robes. And what did they have in their hands? Palms! Let there be no doubt about it, the real palmy days are ahead. One day the shadows of earth will break before the resurrection glory, and the mists of earth will be dispersed by the brightness of heaven. There we will learn that the God who is enough now will be enough throughout all eternity. How could it not be so? So, as the Scottish poet said when contemplating those palmy days in heaven: "Round your faces, the best is yet to be."

Father, I rejoice at the thought that only earth's palmy days are left behind. The real palmy days are ahead. Let the angels be sent forth soon to gather the elect. Even so, come Lord Jesus! Amen.

MANY DO THEIR MOST EFFECTIVE WORK WHEN
THE PRIME OF LIFE IS PAST.

THE DEVIL'S CHIEF WEAPON

"My soul is downcast within me; therefore I will remember you from the land of the Jordan, the heights of Hermon—from Mount Mizar. Deep calls to deep in the roar of your waterfalls; all your waves and breakers have swept over me. By day the LORD directs his love, at night his song is with me—a prayer to the God of my life. I say to God my Rock, 'Why have you forgotten me? Why must I go about mourning, oppressed by the enemy?' My bones suffer mortal agony as my foes taunt me, saying to me all day long, 'Where is your God?' *Why are you downcast, O my soul? Why so disturbed within me? Put your hope in God*, for I will yet praise him, my Savior and my God."

Psalm 42:5–11

As we near the end of our meditations, an important question still remains: Is God enough when we find ourselves in the valley of discouragement and despair? An old Hasidic story goes like this: The devil thought he would retire, believing he had done enough damage to the human race. He decided to give up all his weapons except one—discouragement. He knew that if he ever wanted to come out of retirement, he would still have the weapon he most needed to begin his evil work all over again.

Surrendering Discouragement

One day I visited Southern Ireland to speak at the memorial

service for someone who had been a good friend of mine. At the end of the service, a woman came up to me to let me know how much my writings had ministered to her. She told me she had been a discouraged soul—timid, hesitant, and uncommunicative—until she was given an old copy of *Every Day with Jesus*. In it she read this: "Everyone at times feels the dampening effects of discouragement. The company of the discouraged is not an exclusive club, but it is an expensive club, and in order that you may not find the costs too high, I suggest you turn over your discouragement right now to Jesus. And when you have turned it over, don't take it back." She said: "I used to pray, but had never thought of actually surrendering my discouragement into the hands of Christ and leaving it there. I did just that, and He touched my life in a way I never thought was possible." One of her friends has since informed me that she is now a radiant person— alive and winning many of her friends to Jesus Christ.

Is God enough for those who are discouraged? Again I say, there is no one better. Turn your discouragements over to Him and leave them with Him.

O God, forgive me that I hand over my troubles to You—then take them back again. Help me to give my discouragements to You and leave them with You. In Jesus' Name I pray. Amen.

TURN OVER YOUR DISCOURAGEMENT RIGHT NOW TO JESUS.

"JUST NESTLE"

"Afterward, the prophet came to the king of Israel and said, 'Strengthen your position and see what must be done, because next spring the king of Aram will attack you again.' Meanwhile, the officials of the king of Aram advised him, *'Their gods are gods of the hills.* That is why they were too strong for us. *But if we fight them on the plains, surely we will be stronger than they.* Do this: Remove all the kings from their commands and replace them with other officers. You must also raise an army like the one you lost—horse for horse and chariot for chariot—so we can fight Israel on the plains. Then surely we will be stronger than they.' He agreed with them and acted accordingly."

1 Kings 20:22–25

We continue asking ourselves: Is God enough for us when we find ourselves in the valley of discouragement and despair? Today's passage tells us what the Syrians thought about the God of Israel. They considered that He was limited to helping His people on the hills and that He could not help them in the valleys.

The Syrian army had been roundly defeated following the siege of Samaria. However, the Syrians blamed their defeat on their assumption that the God of the Israelites was essentially a god of the hills and believed this was why He had been successful on the heights of Samaria. In the ancient world, local deities were associated with hills, mountains, streams, and so on, and it seems the Syrians considered the God of the Jews to be a hill-god who would be helpless in the valley. The matter was soon put to the test down on the plains around the city of Aphek, and there God gave the Israelites a victory as decisive as that on the heights of Samaria.

Our All-Sufficient God

However deep is your valley of discouragement, remember that God is the God of the hills and the valleys. There is no situation too big for Him. He is the great *El-Shaddai*, God–the Enough. G. Campbell Morgan, when preaching on the text—"I am God Almighty *[El-Shaddai]*"—said: "The word can be translated 'The Breasted One.' I like that thought. To a baby, a mother is all-sufficient. At her breast the child nestles, draws nourishment and is content." The same is true for the child of God. Ample provision is made through Christ and the Holy Spirit for a believer to draw from the Almighty's sufficiency. So do it. Don't wrestle, just nestle.

O God my Father, teach me how to nestle
in Your arms and draw from You the strength and
power I need to defeat every discouragement.
I know the theory; now help me put what
I know into practice. In Christ's Name. Amen.

THERE IS NO SITUATION TOO BIG FOR GOD.

A N A P O S T L E

I N D E S P A I R

"We do not want you to be uninformed, brothers, about the hardships we suffered in the province of Asia. We *were under great pressure, far beyond our ability to endure, so that we despaired even of life.* Indeed, in our hearts we felt the sentence of death. But this happened that we might not rely on ourselves but on God, who raises the dead. He has delivered us from such a deadly peril, and he will deliver us. On him we have set our hope that he will continue to deliver us, as you help us by your prayers. Then many will give thanks on our behalf for the gracious favor granted us in answer to the prayers of many."

2 Corinthians 1:8–11

Does it surprise you to find the great apostle Paul struggling in the valley of despair? Anyone who finds himself or herself in this position is in good company, for many of the men and women of God in Scripture were also there at one time or another. Paul, having taken gigantic strides into the vast province of Asia, and having forged out an impeccable theology that will serve the Church for all time, reached the lowest point. Weary, lonely, and emotionally drained, the apostle hit bottom.

Can This Be Paul?

The first time I read this passage I thought to myself: "Paul, the hero of the Early Church, in the throes of discouragement and despair? It's unbelievable." Remember what he did at Lystra? A crowd stoned him and left him outside the city, believing him to be dead. But after the disciples had ministered to him, "he got up and went back into the city" (Acts 14:20). Then, after all that, we read: ". . . he and Barnabas left for Derbe." This and other references in Scripture show that Paul was a man of indomitable courage, so why did he reach such a low ebb?

We don't know exactly what reduced him to despair, but we do know that sometimes the most stalwart saints find themselves in a similar situation. Personally, I am deeply grateful for Paul's integrity in recording this incident; otherwise we might think we are inferior Christians if we hover on the verge of despair. I have heard it said: "No Christian should ever be discouraged or allow themselves to be in despair." The theory is fine, but the reality is quite different. The best of Christians can find themselves in the valley of despair. Thankfully, God doesn't let us stay there.

Father, it seems strange to think of the great apostle Paul in despair. But evidently You lifted him out of that condition and restored him to abounding confidence once again. What hope this gives me. I know that whenever I fall victim to despair, You will do the same for me. Thank You, my Father. Amen.

THE BEST OF CHRISTIANS CAN FIND THEMSELVES
IN THE VALLEY OF DESPAIR.

S U R V I V O R S —

B Y   G R A C E

"I rejoice greatly in the Lord that at last you have renewed your concern for me. Indeed, you have been concerned, but you had no opportunity to show it. I am not saying this because I am in need, for I have learned to be content whatever the circumstances. I know what it is to be in need, and I know what it is to have plenty. I have learned the secret of being content in any and every situation, whether well fed or hungry, whether living in plenty or in want. *I can do everything through him who gives me strength.*"

Philippians 4:10–13

Today we ask ourselves: What sort of things bring us down into the valley of discouragement and despair? A Harvard psychologist says that in his experience four things that tip people over into despair are: (1) failure; (2) an unhappy marriage; (3) serious financial difficulties; (4) a serious and incapacitating disease or accident.

Causes of Despair

Take the first—*failure*. Some would say that Jesus' life was a failure. A cross spells failure whichever way you look at it. But this overlooks the fact of a living God who is able to take failure and turn it into something that contributes.

A friend of mine, a Christian counselor, has three suggestions when helping people who are faced with failure. First, analyze the situation carefully (perhaps with the help of a friend) to discover how things went wrong. Second, consider the worst possible scenario. Third, put your hand in the hand of God, pray for continued guidance, and devote yourself to moving on in a close relationship with Him. No failure is failure if it succeeds in driving us closer to the Lord.

Then what about an *unhappy marriage*? God can, if you let Him, come very close to you in such a situation. Stop thinking that your husband or wife provides the basis for your emotional security—God does. Don't try to change your partner through nagging or by the use of threats. Examine your own heart to see how you have contributed to the problem, ask forgiveness for that, and leave God to make the difference. This may not change your marriage, but it can change you. And that is the secret. I know many people with unhappy marriages who still function well because of their rich relationship with the Lord.

O God my Father, forgive me that I struggle to survive by drawing on my own resources rather than on Yours. Help me grasp that when I draw upon Your grace and power, I do not merely survive— I thrive. Thank You, my Father. Amen.

NO FAILURE IS FAILURE IF IT SUCCEEDS IN BRINGING US CLOSER TO THE LORD.

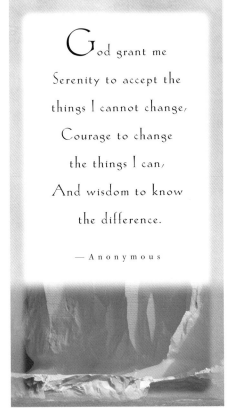

God grant me
Serenity to accept the
things I cannot change,
Courage to change
the things I can,
And wisdom to know
the difference.

— Anonymous

GOD The Enough

KEEP GRACE
FLOWING

God's love cannot be portioned
out in quantities nicely adjusted
to the merits of individuals.
There is such a thing as the
twelfth part of a denarius . . .
but there is no such thing as a
twelfth part of the love of God.

— T. W. Manson

"A SECRET STAIR..."

"Why do you say, O Jacob, and complain, O Israel, 'My way is hidden from the LORD; my cause is disregarded by my God'? Do you not know? Have you not heard? The LORD is an everlasting God, the Creator of the ends of the earth. He will not grow tired or weary, and his understanding no one can fathom. *He gives strength to the weary and increases the power of the weak.* Even youths grow tired and weary, and young men stumble and fall; but those who hope in the LORD will renew their strength. They will soar on wings like eagles; they will run and not grow weary, they will walk and not be faint."

Isaiah 40:27–31

We continue looking at the four things a Harvard psychologist says tip people over into discouragement and despair. He lists the third as *serious financial difficulties.* How can God be sufficient when you have major money problems?

There are many ways in which the Lord can work to help people in such distress. One, He can touch the heart of someone with financial resources and inspire them to help. Two, He can bring about a change of circumstances—a new job, an increase in salary, and so on. Three, He can impart wisdom and courage to the person concerned so that he or she asks some searching questions to find a way out. A person in financial difficulty needs to face up to such questions as these: Have I overspent? Has my heart run away with my head? Most times it is not money but the management of it that is the problem. A friend of mine, a financial expert, when counseling someone in financial difficulties, begins not by talking about money but about personal issues. "Money management," he says, "is self-management."

Dejection

What about the fourth cause of dejection—*a serious and incapacitating disease or accident?* Many people reach despair when a disease or accident disables them, preventing them from contributing to life. Can God minister to people in this condition and keep them blithe if not blissful? Only those who find themselves in this condition can answer such a question. And what do they say? A friend of mine, crippled by polio, answered for all who find Christ's grace sufficient: "In all things God finds a secret stair to the soul, and what we lack in movement of the body we make up for in the movement of the soul."

Father, I see that self-management comes before the management of things. Help me curb any worldly desires I have that may be leading me into difficulty. For Jesus' sake. Amen.

"MONEY MANAGEMENT IS SELF-MANAGEMENT."

LIFE'S GREATEST LESSON

"Watch out for those dogs, those men who do evil, those mutilators of the flesh. For it is we who are the circumcision, we who worship by the Spirit of God, who glory in Christ Jesus, and who put no confidence in the flesh— though I myself have reasons for such confidence. *If anyone else thinks he has reasons to put confidence in the flesh, I have more*: circumcised on the eighth day, of the people of Israel, of the tribe of Benjamin, a Hebrew of Hebrews; in regard to the law, a Pharisee; as for zeal, persecuting the church; as for legalistic righteousness, faultless. But whatever was to my profit I now consider loss for the sake of Christ. What is more, I consider everything a loss compared to the surpassing greatness of knowing Christ Jesus my Lord, for whose sake I have lost all things."

Philippians 3:2–8a

In reflecting on our theme, God–the Enough, our emphasis has been on the fact that whatever the situation in which we find ourselves, there is enough in God—indeed *more than enough*—to get us through. The old hymn says: "Grace is flowing like a river." While this is true, we need to ask: How do we ensure that it flows into our hearts? What does it take to let grace in? That is the issue with which we come to grips in this final section.

Paul the Perfect

Permit me to turn your attention to the apostle Paul once again. In our passage today he tells us that he put no confidence in the flesh. Look closely at his credentials again: he was circumcised; one of the people of Israel; as far as keeping the law was concerned, a Pharisee, zealous, faultless. Paul was the perfect Pharisee. No one could find a flaw in his commitment to the law. "That's my record," claims Paul. But he goes on to declare that he considers all of those things rubbish that he may gain Christ. Do you follow what he is saying? "I have lost confidence in my track record, my pedigree, my press reports. My hope and trust now is in the Lord Jesus Christ. He is enough."

The secret of availing ourselves of God's grace is to have more confidence in God than we do in ourselves. During an interview for a television program in Canada, I was asked: "Selwyn, you have a lifetime of experience in serving Christ. What is the most important lesson you have learned?" This was my reply: "Dependency. Life works better when you throw all your weight on Christ. Not part of your weight, not even a lot of your weight. All your weight."

O God, teach me how to throw my whole weight upon You. Forgive me that so often my trust is in other things plus You. Show me that without You other things would be of no use whatsoever. First and foremost, I must recognize that You are "the Enough." Amen.

THE SECRET OF AVAILING OURSELVES OF GOD'S GRACE IS TO HAVE MORE CONFIDENCE IN GOD THAN WE DO IN OURSELVES.

GOD'S PURPOSE

"If, while we seek to be justified in Christ, it becomes evident that we ourselves are sinners, does that mean that Christ promotes sin? Absolutely not! If I rebuild what I destroyed, I prove that I am a lawbreaker. For through the law I died to the law so that I might live for God. I have been crucified with Christ and I no longer live, but Christ lives in me. The life I live in the body, I live by faith in the Son of God, who loved me and gave himself for me. *I do not set aside the grace of God*, for if righteousness could be gained through the law, Christ died for nothing!"

Galatians 2:17–21

We are now drawing our thoughts to a close with the question: We know there is enough grace in God to meet every need of ours, but how do we open ourselves to it? Yesterday we concluded that the secret is to have more confidence in God than we do in ourselves. Yet in our text for today, we find Paul saying: "I do not set aside the grace of God." So clearly, then, there is the danger that we can distance ourselves from God's grace. One translation puts it: "I do not frustrate the grace of God. . ." (KJV).

Frustrating God's Grace

How can we frustrate God's grace? By depending on something other than grace to accomplish God's purposes in our lives. This is the point Paul is making in the passage: if we could be saved by some means other than the grace of God expressed through Christ's sacrifice on the cross, then "Christ died for nothing." We frustrate God's grace when we try to achieve the divine end without using the divine method. It was said of the Pharisees that they "rejected God's purpose for themselves" (Luke 7:30). The purpose of God for them was repentance and baptism by John.

What is God's purpose for us? It is that we should allow Him to enter our lives through the act of repentance and become dependent each day on the resources of His grace. Some think that dependency on God involves disregarding their skills, their education, their abilities, and so on. Not so. Dependency means that first and foremost our trust is in God. He is not going to ignore our training, our abilities, our knowledge, or our experience—but He wants to be the chief resource. Our talents and gifts are far more effective when they are energized by His grace.

Father, thank You for all the gifts and graces
You have given me. Show me that to depend on
You is not to demean me but to develop me, not to hurt
me or limit me but help me. In Jesus' Name. Amen.

DEPENDENCY MEANS THAT FIRST AND FOREMOST
OUR TRUST IS IN GOD.

INSPIRED SAINTS

"Therefore, I urge you, brothers, in view of God's mercy, to offer your bodies as living sacrifices, holy and pleasing to God—this is your spiritual act of worship. Do not conform any longer to the pattern of this world, but be transformed by the renewing of your mind. Then you will be able to test and approve what God's will is—his good, pleasing and perfect will. For by the grace given me I say to every one of you: Do not think of yourself more highly than you ought, but *rather think of yourself with sober judgment, in accordance with the measure of faith God has given you.* Just as each of us has one body with many members, and these members do not all have the same function, so in Christ we who are many form one body, and each member belongs to all the others."

Romans 12: 1—5

As we acknowledged yesterday, God's purpose is to bring us into such a close relationship with Himself that we draw each day on His grace. And it is only when we fulfill God's purpose that we fulfill ourselves. We must not be afraid of this truth. It goes against our nature, I know, because we fear giving up our autonomy. Yet oh, if only we could see that when we are His, fully His, we are most ourselves. Bound to Him, we walk the earth free. Low at His feet, we stand tall over everything.

Ananias and Sapphira

We also noted yesterday that God had a purpose for the Pharisees, but they preferred another way. God's purpose for

Ananias and Sapphira was frustrated when they kept back part of the proceeds of the sale of their land while pretending to give the whole amount (see Acts 5:1–11). They gave, but they didn't give *all*. Did they fear, I wonder, that God would not take care of them and would let them down? Whatever it was, they did not throw their whole weight on God and thus thwarted His purposes. In contrast, Barnabas gave all he had and walked into the future with his head held high (see Acts 4:36–37). His example has inspired the saints throughout the ages.

We either fulfill the purpose of God or frustrate it. His purpose is to bring us into a relationship with Himself and maintain that relationship by getting us to draw upon His everlasting grace. But doesn't this make us passive and dependent? Doesn't depending on Another take away our confidence in ourselves? No, rather the reverse. It increases confidence by imparting to us Christ's confidence. We take our place in Him, and He takes His place in us.

O Father, thank You for reminding me that dependency does not mean passivity. The more I draw on Your grace the more fully my gifts and talents can be expressed. Impart the confidence of Your Son into my life so that I become more Christ-confident than self-confident. For His dear Name's sake. Amen.

LOW AT HIS FEET, WE STAND TALL OVER EVERYTHING.

"I Did It My Way"

"John replied, 'A man can receive only what is given him from heaven. You yourselves can testify that I said, "I am not the Christ but am sent ahead of him." The bride belongs to the bridegroom. The friend who attends the bridegroom waits and listens for him, and is full of joy when he hears the bridegroom's voice. That joy is mine, and it is now complete. *He must become greater; I must become less.* The one who comes from above is above all; the one who is from the earth belongs to the earth, and speaks as one from the earth. The one who comes from heaven is above all.'"

John 3:27–31

It takes a great deal of humility to depend on God and to go through life drawing upon His grace each day. Our nature (a legacy from Adam) causes us to want to walk independently of God and say with Frank Sinatra: "I did it my way." When will we see that we have been made to walk in step with another, to live in daily fellowship with God, and to draw upon His rich resources? We must stop trying to impress people with our own prowess.

The job description of a Christian is, as John puts it in our text for today, to let Him become greater and let ourselves become less. I used to shrink from these words because there was something in me that wanted it to be the other way around. I was perfectly willing to let Christ decrease as long as I increased—increased in reputation and prominence.

The biggest battle of my life has been to put personal ambition behind Christ rather than in front of Him, and it is not so long ago that I realized the battle had been won. Someone asked me in an interview: "Would you be willing, if it was God's will, to give up writing *Every Day with Jesus* and allow your name to sink into oblivion?" I thought for a moment and said: "If that was what God wanted, it would be fine with me." Some years ago I could not have said that, but realizing I had reached that point gave me great joy.

Challenge

I've told you my weakness—what about yours? Is there some independent streak that God is making you conscious of right now? Ask yourself: Is there anything I wouldn't give up for Him? It takes great humility to say: "He must become greater; I must become less." But once we show we are willing, God then shows us His power.

Father, forgive me if I strut through life like a
prima donna, trying to draw attention to myself.
Give me the humility and sense of daily dependence
that characterized the life of Your Son.
For His dear Name's sake I ask it. Amen.

WE MUST STOP TRYING TO IMPRESS PEOPLE
WITH OUR OWN PROWESS.

OUR ONE
REQUIREMENT

"It was good of you to share in my troubles. Moreover, as you Philippians know, in the early days of your acquaintance with the gospel, when I set out from Macedonia, not one church shared with me in the matter of giving and receiving, except you only; for even when I was in Thessalonica, you sent me aid again and again when I was in need. Not that I am looking for a gift, but I am looking for what may be credited to your account. I have received full payment and even more; I am amply supplied, now that I have received from Epaphroditus the gifts you sent. They are a fragrant offering, an acceptable sacrifice, pleasing to God. *And my God will meet all your needs according to his glorious riches in Christ Jesus."*

Philippians 4:14—19

On this, the penultimate day of our reflections on the theme "God—the Enough," I want to take a moment to remind you of what we have been saying. God is sufficient in every sphere, but most wonderfully in the realm of grace. There is grace for sin, there is grace for suffering, and there is grace for service.

Illusory Thinking

We consider we do not have enough of much in this world— money, friends, prestige, education, and so on. People often think that if they had enough of these things, then they would be happy. But such thinking is illusory. The real trouble is not that people don't have enough of these things but that these things in themselves are not enough. If we had everything we craved and yet did not have God, then we would not have enough. We would still be conscious of desires unmet and longings unfulfilled.

In my native country, Wales, we have a saying: *Heb Dduw; Heb Ddim,* which means: "Without God, Without Anything." Henry Van Dyke once expressed this same point in these words: "There is absolutely nothing that man cannot do without—except God." The Almighty alone is sufficient for us. We can get by without social standing, wealth, and a whole host of other things, but we cannot get by without God. Do you realize that? Have you grasped its implications? Only He is sufficient for us; only He can really satisfy our souls. No one but the eternal God is enough. This has been our constant emphasis throughout our meditations. Now we must let it sink in.

Father, You have hammered home this truth
in one way and another over many days and weeks.
Now let it control my thinking and all my
attitudes, not only today but all the days of my life.
In Christ's Name. Amen.

WITHOUT GOD, WITHOUT ANYTHING.

GRACE BE WITH YOU

"So then, dear friends, since you are looking forward to this, make every effort to be found spotless, blameless and at peace with him. Bear in mind that our Lord's patience means salvation, just as our dear brother Paul also wrote you with the wisdom that God gave him. He writes the same way in all his letters, speaking in them of these matters. His letters contain some things that are hard to understand, which ignorant and unstable people distort, as they do the other Scriptures, to their own destruction. Therefore, dear friends, since you already know this, be on your guard so that you may not be carried away by the error of lawless men and fall from your secure position. *But grow in the grace and knowledge of our Lord and Savior Jesus Christ.* To him be glory both now and forever! Amen."

2 Peter 3:14–18

We come now to the end of our meditations on the theme "God—the Enough." What does the immediate future hold for us, I wonder? I can tell you this: it will be wonderful for those who know how to depend on God's grace. The economy may fail, there may be drought or floods, but one thing is sure: God will never run out of supplies of grace.

Enough and to Spare

And here's another exciting thing: As you receive grace, you will be able to show more and more grace to others. Only when you model it will you realize just how amazing it is. Among the most beautiful of Paul's words are these: "Remember I am in prison. Grace be with you" (Col. 4:18 MOFFATT).

Wouldn't you have expected Paul to say: "I am in prison, pray that God will give me grace"? But no, he says something quite different: "I am in prison. Grace be with you." When the prodigal son was hungry, he remembered that in his father's house not only was there just enough food but there was "bread enough and to spare" (Luke 15:17 KJV). Similarly, in prison Paul found grace and to spare. It is as if he is saying: "God's grace is more than sufficient in this jail. There is so much that I pass it on to you."

I would like to let a Welsh hymnist, John Matthews, have the last word in our meditations. Here, in these lovely lines, he seems to sum up all we have been saying:

Its streams the whole creation reach
So plenteous is its store,
Enough for all, enough for each,
Enough for evermore.
Enough!

O Father, if my circumstances are difficult, then help me see there is grace enough and to spare. Help me not to complain but to draw on Your resources. For I know that grace is sufficient not only when I am happy and free but when the hardships of life trap me and I feel as if I am in prison. I shall find grace even then. Amen.

ENOUGH FOREVERMORE.

Amazing grace!
how sweet
the sound
That saved a wretch
like me!
I once was lost,
but now am found,
Was blind,
but now I see.

— John Newton

GOD The Enough

AUSTRALIA: CMC Australasia
P.O. Box 519, Belmont, Victoria 3216 Tel: (03) 5241 3288

CANADA: CMC Distribution Ltd.
P.O. Box 7000, Niagara on the Lake, Ontario L0S 1J0 Tel: 1 800 325 1297

INDIA: Full Gospel Literature Stores
254 Kilpauk Garden Road, Chennai 600010 Tel: (44) 644 3073

KENYA: Keswick Bookshop
P.O. Box 10242, Nairobi Tel: (02) 331692/226047

MALAYSIA: Salvation Book Centre (M)
23 Jalan SS2/64, Sea Park, 47300 Petaling Jaya, Selangor Tel: (3) 7766411

NEW ZEALAND: CMC New Zealand Ltd.
P.O. Box 949, 205 King Street South, Hastings
Tel: (6) 8784408, Toll free: 0800 333639

NIGERIA: FBFM (Every Day with Jesus)
Prince's Court, 37 Ahmed Onibudo Street, P.O. Box 70952, Victoria Island
Tel: 01 2617721, 616832, 4700218

REPUBLIC OF IRELAND: Scripture Union
40 Talbot Street, Dublin 1 Tel: (01) 8363764

SINGAPORE: Campus Crusade Asia Ltd.
315 Outram Road, 06–08 Tan Boon Liat Building, Singapore 169074
Tel: (65) 222 3640

SOUTH AFRICA: Struik Christian Books (Pty Ltd)
P.O. Box 193, Maitland 7405, Cape Town Tel: (021) 551 5900

SRI LANKA: Christombu Investments
27 Hospital Street, Colombo 1 Tel: (1) 433142/328909

USA: CMC Distribution
P.O. Box 644, Lewiston, New York 14092–0644 Tel: 1 800 325 1297